FINANCING
ELECTIONS

FINANCING
ELECTIONS

THE POLITICS
OF AN AMERICAN
RULING CLASS

DAVID NICHOLS

NEW VIEWPOINTS
A Division of Franklin Watts, Inc.
New York | 1974

Text design by Scott Chelius
Cover design by Nick Krenitsky

Library of Congress Cataloging in Publication Data

Nichols, David, 1940–
    Financing elections.

    Includes bibliographical references.
    1. Elections–United States–Campaign funds.
2. Business and politics–United States. I. Title.
JK1991.N5   329′.025   73-3420
ISBN 0-531-05352-0
ISBN 0-531-05553-1 (pbk.)

CONTENTS

TO CAROL

preface

Some people will like this book, others not, but
few will feel neutral about it. It is my hope that
even those who begin it and find they dislike
it will keep on reading angrily away. Sometimes
I have found that I recall, years after the fact,
books that had made me furious when I first
read them. It usually turns out that these works
had irritated me because they had gotten down
to basics I wasn't ready to confront. Yet the fundamental issues they had raised eventually in-

truded into my political thinking, and in having to take account of them I benefited intellectually.

One of the maddening treatises to which I have returned several times is Milton Friedman's *Capitalism and Freedom*. Friedman's chief purpose, it seemed to me, was to find a moral justification for the inequalities that are inherent in a capitalist society. Unlike the vast majority of writings that accept our social order, Friedman confronted a basic issue explicitly and squarely: the justifying principle which the economist located for capitalism was individual freedom.

Thinking about the solution offered by Friedman helped me to realize that, in truth, inequality is immoral, and that its existence neither springs from nor in turn guarantees individual freedom.

One of the passages in *Capitalism and Freedom* which had particularly bothered me is related to the subject of this book:

> In a capitalist society, it is only necessary to convince a few wealthy people to get funds to launch any idea, however strange, and there are many such persons, many independent foci of support.[1]

To explain what is wrong with this formulation, deceptively simple though it seems at first glance, I found would take a book—this book. Like Friedman, we began with the basics. It was once observed that "no people can be free in any real sense of the word who do not retain control of the economic structure of their country." [2] Indeed, a nation's political system cannot be free and democratic while its economic system is unfree and undemocratic. The primary reason for the impossibility of such a state of affairs lies in the fact that the economic system is part of the political system. That is, the control of the means of production and distribution of goods—control of

the economy on which we all depend—is by definition political in character.

The election financing system reflects the "economic" political power structure and, in turn, feeds
back in to this economic dictatorship in a supportive
way. In this book I examine the relationship of campaign finance to the system of power in U.S. society.
This means that this book is first and foremost an
analysis of political power.

Several people were of assistance to me at various
stages in this project, though some of them will not
agree with the analysis presented here. Roldo Barti-
mole, Gordon Corlew, David Gold, G. William Domhoff, Edward Gelbman, David Gorka, Steven Green-
wald, Margaret MacDowell, Kenny Zapp, and Mike
Zweig helped in different ways. Especially important
help came from Ray Nakabayashi. The same is true
of Clifford Solway, whose idea the book was.

FINANCING ELECTIONS

the real problem

A ruling class has developed in America. The democratic aspect of American society is of great importance, but it is nevertheless a secondary aspect. Democracy's opposite, a class power structure, is the dominant aspect of the U.S. social system today.

The economic process on which we all depend is increasingly dominated by a small class of people who control the major economic corporations. This small group *is the ruling class.* "Rule" is a political term. Because corporate economic decisions affect us all and are backed by legal authority, they are in fact *political* decisions. Any class that dominates our economic process is engaged in the activity of political rule.

But there is more to the class power structure: the economic class that rules politically through corporations *also* dominates the formally democratic governmental structure of the United States.

It is our broad purpose in this book to contribute to the analysis of how a relatively very small social class manages to rule effectively over millions of people. The particular aspect of the system of political rule which we shall single out for closer examination in this book is the election financing process.

Under present circumstances financing elections is one of the more important types of political activity in which members of the social elite engage. The day is not far off when the total spent on all campaigns in just one election year will be more than a half-billion dollars. The obvious implications of campaign funding— to which most people do not contribute, and to which a few fat cats contribute very heavily indeed—are not lost on informed observers. "It is almost impossible for a poor man to run for public office and . . . a man of moderate means can do so only if he has the backing of men and forces of great wealth," complained former U.S. Senator Paul H. Douglas in 1967 Senate testimony.[1]

Costs are seldom low in a campaign for an important office; 70 percent of a sample of Senators recently interviewed by the Special Committee on Congressional Ethics of the New York City Bar Association admitted having spent over $100,000 in their last general election campaign.[2] Costs are often very high. In 1970, for example, Washington columnists Evans and Novak confidently anticipated a Democratic Senatorial primary victory in Ohio for ex-astronaut John Glenn. A poll had shown that Glenn was known to almost all Ohio voters while his opponent, millionaire labor lawyer Howard Metzenbaum, was known to but a fraction.[3] But Glenn was short of cash, and Metzenbaum's organization spent almost a million dollars in a television blitz that defeated Glenn.[4] (Metzenbaum went on to lose to fellow millionaire Robert Taft, Jr., in the general election.)

Metzenbaum's outlays were far from unique; in neighboring Pennsylvania in the same year, millionaire Milton J. Shapp spent a million dollars in the Democratic primary (his campaigns in the 1966 primary and general elections had cost almost $4 million) and went on to win the gubernatorial election. Yet Shapp's 1970 primary costs worked out to $2.30 per vote cast for him, considerably less than the $11 per vote cost of New York real estate developer James H. Scheuer's successful campaign for a House nomination that year.[5]

As the costs of campaigns mount, absolutely and relative to price increases, many reformers have been talking about such matters as (1) the problem of the poor man's ability to run for office, (2) the problem of the effect of expenditures on which candidate wins, and (3) the problem of big contributors to campaign funds pressing for special governmental favors after a victory by their man. As real as these problems are, however, the way in which they are posed shows that reformers seldom see the deeper and most crucial significance of financing. A partial exception is Senator Douglas, who stated:

> A Congress or an executive branch largely composed of men of great wealth or of their protégés will inevitably become a class-dominated legislature in which the crucial decisions will predominately be made in favor of the interests of the affluent.[6]

But even Senator Douglas shrank from the obvious conclusion that, given the admitted economic prerequisites of running for major office, there already *is* a class-dominated government in America.

ECONOMICS AND POLITICS

Control of the economic process on which we all depend for a living is not an economic question separate from the realm of politics, but rather the most important political question of the 1970's. Indeed, the politics of economic control have been the most important underlying politics of man's short history.

In the United States, power in production and distribution has for some time been concentrated in the hands of a relatively very small social class of people who own and control the major corporations that dominate the economy. Since the corporate controllers reap the material benefits of their power positions, they may be called, after C. Wright Mills, *the corporate rich.*[7]

Corporate power cannot be long exercised unless sanctioned by that institution we call the state or the government, which uses authority backed by armed force to maintain the structure of the social system. In contemporary America, it has become increasingly evident that the corporate rich have a grip on the state that effectively prevents any political challenge to their social position. The upper class in society thus enjoys governmental as well as corporate power; the corporate rich are an economic class that rule politically.[8]

The political power of the corporate rich, like all such power, is relational. That is, it involves mutual interactions—relationships—between rulers and ruled. Power is not just something the authorities have; it is something they possess conditional upon some minimum level of popular submission to their rule.

One means of securing popular submission is quite straightforward: the national state has armed force at its disposal and its use or threatened use is an essential ingredient of law enforcement. This armed force is at the ultimate disposal of the group that effectively controls the national government; today it constitutes a major means of maintaining class rule.

Even more important than armed force in political rule is the people's sense of whether or not the governing group has a right to rule. In connection with the struggle to influence the minds of people politically, the domination of corporate influence in major opinion-shaping institutions—including corporate control of the principal means of political communication (the mass media)—constitutes a second major means of securing submission to class rule. This is not, of course, a straightforward process, for it operates through the medium of a democratic—free enterprise ideology that obscures what is actually happening in contemporary America.

Most people spend most of their waking lives in the struggle to make a living. For their jobs they usually depend on bosses responsible to corporate controllers. Engaging in political action—at work and in the community—brings with it the real risk of employer dissatisfaction should the action seem deleterious to him or to the corporate system. The right to hire and fire is a political power, anyway, but it can also be used to maintain itself—that is, as a third major means of political control.

The structure of the government also operates to

maintain the system of power. American governmental structure probably renders it impossible for any potential political party aiming to vest control of the society in the people themselves to win power through the electoral process. In some major countries, where a single national election decides who controls the parliament (and, with it, the entire government), electoral power revolution is a structural possibility. But the structure of government in the United States is fragmented. There are two houses of Congress, separately elected, and a separately elected President, and all have independent legislative power (they "check and balance" each other). Ordinarily seen as a virtue in schoolbooks, the fact is that once the basic interests of the corporate rich become incorporated into the diverse parts of government, the fragmented check-and-balance system makes it virtually impossible to effectively dislodge them through elections. Involved are many governments within one—courts, departments, commissions, and legislatures at national and subnational levels—which have meshed their activities with the basic requirements of the corporate control system.

Election financing, finally, is one of the several major means by which the political power position of the corporate rich is maintained. The principal effects of this financing are on what political scientists like to call the political recruitment process—namely, the process by which people come to hold governmental office.

ELECTION FINANCING AND CLASS RULE

Two points about our intention to explore campaign financing as an aspect of ruling class politics should be clear by now. First, election financing is seen not as a problem of malfunctioning democracy but as a *func-*

tional part of a substantially nondemocratic social system. And second, election financing is seen as *but one of the means by which the class power position of the corporate rich is maintained.* There are several major (and many minor) means of system maintenance, and our focus on campaign funding is not intended to deny the great importance of other conservative forces.

Now, the reader may have some doubts about our aim, so clarified. First, he may wonder whether some major reform, recent or incipient, will knock out campaign funding as a cornerstone of the existing system. During the age of television, which since the mid-1950's has occasioned a relative rise in campaign costs, there has been much public discussion of financing as a problem of democracy. Reformers (and also party politicians pressed for funds) have aired their complaints in Congress. Legislation has been proposed; some of it has been enacted.

Yet neither the articulation of the problem nor the enacting of reforms is really very new. A professor commenting on the ineffectiveness of legislation on the books once wrote:

> *In response to public pressure Congress has enacted various laws regulating the use of money in federal elections, while many of the state legislatures have done likewise for state elections. But for fourteen years, in spite of frequent and prominent discussions of the question, no real advance has been made; we are in very much the same position now that we were in fourteen years ago.*[9]

These words were written in 1926—after a major law bearing on campaign finance (the Corrupt Practices Act of 1925) had been passed—by James Pollock, Jr., a pioneer student of election financing. They have a remarkably contemporary ring. The "problem," it appears, is as old as the coincidence of mass democracy with industrial capitalism: it dates at least from the

1880's. If the precise uses for which money is spent have changed over time—the outright buying of votes is largely a historical curiosity, while the selling of candidates via television is a distinctly modern expense —the raising of big money has remained a constant, inherent in the system, throughout the period.

Can we expect more from the reform legislation signed into law in 1971 than Professor Pollock expected from the reform legislation of 1925? So far as the basic patterns of election financing are concerned, the answer, as we shall show, has to be "no." The new laws were drawn up, after all, by the existing class-dominated government. We will show that no reform either on the books or recently proposed within the present government has offered the prospect of eliminating the dependence of major candidates upon private wealth. No mere law is about to change the essential reality described in this book.

The reader may have a second and more fundamental question about our aim in this book: What does it mean to say that the corporate rich are a ruling class? It means, primarily, that this very small group in society *controls most of the resources, facilities, tools, and machines needed to produce and distribute the goods* that are the basis of social life; this control is realized through appropriate types of institutions—most immediately, corporations. Further, though there is mobility in and out of the upper class over time, this control of access to the means by which work can produce useful things is passed on through generations.

To say that the corporate rich are a ruling class also means that they have a collective *dominance within the government such that (at a minimum) no major policy of the national state jeopardizes the corporate system from which they benefit* (and benefit materially and mightily). The state has become one of the institutions through which control of the productive system is realized; the acts of government are in conformity with the interests of the elite.

If the policies of the American government merely protected the corporate system in the minimum way just mentioned, their consequences would be deleterious enough for the majority of people, for by far most people are wage-and-salary workers in the corporate system, and powerlessness and economic insecurity demonstrably accompany their work situation. Most major policies are, however, designed to do more than merely enforce "capitalism." Most policies positively benefit either the entire corporate system, or a particular set of corporations. To benefit corporations is to benefit the corporate rich, for these people's wealth, prestige, and power are rooted in the economic institutions that they control. In benefiting corporations, the policies of government usually fail to benefit working people. The puzzlingly negative popular effects of tax policy, war policy, and, indeed, of law enforcement and social policy generally become more comprehensible when seen as logical consequences of a system of class rule.

All previous books on campaign financing save one have been written with the explicit or implicit assumption that we live in a democratic society, albeit an imperfect democracy.[10] Almost all U.S. writers on election financing have called the fact of private money a problem of democratic politics, as if a genuine democratic politics already existed. This, however, is precisely what is questioned. And financing itself actually implies plutocracy—governance of and for the rich. But because financing facts themselves do not and cannot prove the existence of plutocracy (or democracy or any other power structure), an intelligent determination of the meaning of the huge amounts of private cash spent in the electoral process *requires* a separate consideration of the character of power in America.

THE REAL PROBLEM

Subsequent to our analysis of this power structure, which follows, we can return to election financing and explore its complex role relative to the political realities—not the schoolbook myths—of American society.

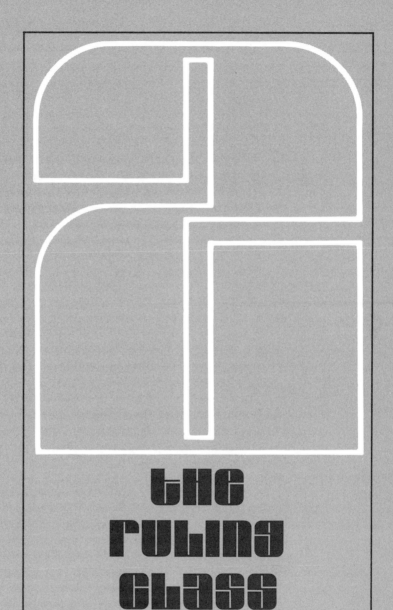

the
ruling
class

DEFINITIONS

If we lived in a democratic society, all individuals would have roughly equal influence over the social decisions that affected their lives. No groups or individuals would have any special vested degree of control over any areas of social life, and people generally would be agreed on broad principles of equity in socioeconomic arrangements. We do not live in a democratic society, nor have many people lived very long in a democratic society in the course of human history. Democracy remains an unrealized ideal, and its achievement will be possible only if the vast majority of people begin to understand how far we are from it and if, as a consequence of that understanding, they begin to strive for a democratic way of life.

To understand society as it really is, we must begin with the human decisions that have the most important effects on the largest numbers of people. These are, in general, made in what we call the economic realm. Most people in the world and in this society, even at this late date in human history, are still primarily involved in the struggle to ensure their physical survival and comfort. We spend most of our time, directly or indirectly, in the enterprise of making a living. The decisions that affect our "economic" fate are, normally, more really and immediately important to us than any others. Objectively, their impact on our physical and psychological well-being is certainly greater than the ordinary impact of other types of decisions.

The means by which people live are, in the first place, the tools, techniques, facilities, and resources through which creative labor is applied to yield the necessaries of human life. Yet human history has seen *control* of the means by which people live (and thereby, of the fruits of people's labor) lodged in successive minorities who have been able to set self-serving preconditions on people's right to work. Only during exceptional episodes in history, thus far, have the many been able to wrest control of the means by which they live from the few.

The few who control the means by which men live may be called the ruling class, following a definition offered some years ago by James Burnham in *The Managerial Revolution:*

In most types of society that we know about, and in all complex societies so far, there is a particular, and relatively small, group of men that controls the chief instruments of production (a control which is summed up legally in the concept of "property right," though it is not the legal concept but the fact of control which concerns us). This control (property right) is never absolute; it is always subject to certain limitations or restrictions (as, for instance, against using the objects controlled to murder others at will) which vary in kind and degree. The crucial phases of this control seem to be two: first, the ability, either through personal strength, or, as in complex societies, with the backing— threatened or actual—of the state power acting through the police, courts, and armed forces to prevent access by others to the objects controlled (owned); and, second, a preferential treatment in the distribution of the products of the objects controlled (owned).

Where there is such a controlling group in society, a group which, as against the rest of society, has a greater measure of control over the access to the instruments of production and a preferential treatment in the distribution of the products of those instruments, we may speak of this group as the socially dominant or ruling class in that society. It is hard, indeed, to see what else could be meant by "dominant" or "ruling" class. Such a group has the power and privilege and wealth in the society, as against the remainder of society. It will be noted that this definition of a ruling class does not presuppose any particular kind of government or any particular legal form of property right; it rests upon the facts of control of access and preferential treatment, and can be investigated empirically.[1]

Empirically, the broad legal and practical realities are such that most of the economic activity of contemporary American capitalism falls under the control of those who have owning interests as proprietors or (more usually) as corporate officers and directors in the mines, factories, railroads, land, etc., that constitute the means of production. These, the capitalists, hire the labor of others to create useful things with these resources, but the legal ownership and actual control of the products of such labor remain with the capitalists.

It would be correct to call capitalists the ruling class, following Burnham's definition, were it not for the fact that the vast majority of capitalists control a residual portion of the economic apparatus, while a tiny fraction of them control the great bulk of the productive system. It seems increasingly necessary to distinguish among capitalists, and to reserve the designation "ruling class" for those who control the big financial and industrial corporations that effectively dominate the economy.

The rise of a class of big capitalists controlling powerful corporations in a nationalized industrial economy occurred in the closing decades of the last century. The business class as a whole shrank, and came to embody men whose interests converged on some fundamentals but diverged on other matters.

All businessmen, big and small, adhere to what we euphemistically call free enterprise. In other words, they share an economic interest in profit-making. The basic characteristic of capitalism is private control of the means of producing and distributing commodities, *and* the consequent need of many (in fact, an increasing majority) to sell their time to those who control the workplaces.[2] It is from this relationship that businessmen's profits are derived. Preserving this profit system in some form is a common interest of the business class.

But the corporate rich are a class of people whose past, present, and future business it is to be directors of the big corporations that dominate the economy. These businessmen—and, socially, their families—have a distinctive vested interest in the maintenance of the economic power of the big corporations. Long ago there were serious political struggles between small and large businessmen, and the former lost quite decisively.[3] Today the small businessman tends to identify with the world of business as such.[4] Yet the powerful corporate rich are but a small segment of the whole business class.

It is not yet possible to identify the corporate rich with numerical precision, for there is no sudden leap from small to giant business. Adolph Berle recently noted that at least four-fifths of total business activity is carried on by the top 3,500 of America's more than one million corporations.[5] John Kenneth Galbraith, noting that in 1962 the 500 largest industrial corporations had more than two-thirds of all assets used in manufacturing, argued that the 200 largest corporations occupy the "industrial heartland" of the economy.[6]

Major banking, insurance, industrial, and other corporations are not neatly separated from one another. The biggest companies virtually always hold stock in other firms, large or small. Increasingly, directors of big corporations hold directorships in more than one company. The resulting interlocking directorates are an institutional feature of growing importance.[7] Corporations interlock with each other (and with foundations and universities), and these interlocks are clues to the internal financial interest groups of the corporate world. G. William Domhoff has synthesized important indications that these financial interest groups are centered on major banks.[8] Competition among corporate groupings for larger shares of the economy is an important aspect of big capitalism. This competition is, of course, predicated upon the continued health of the big corporate world as a whole.

It is evident, then, that "there is a national corporate economy that is run by the same group of several thousand men." [9] An exact specification of the corporate rich will have to await a more thorough study of the guts of high capitalism. But the class that controls the biggest corporations is probably contained somewhere within the less than 1 percent of the population that owns most of the corporate stock.[10] As an approximate economic indicator of membership among the corporate rich, the most useful readily available tool is the list of top U.S. companies issued annually in *Fortune* Magazine. *Fortune,* essentially a magazine of and for the corporate rich and their agents, lists the top 1,000 industrial corporations and the top 50 each of banks, insurance companies, utilities, transportation companies, and retailing companies. Some companies in unlisted fields are comparable in size to those on the *Fortune* lists.

The corporate rich can be seen, in the first place, as the senior officers and members of the boards of directors of the companies in the annual *Fortune* lists and of other firms comparable in size. In the second place, the corporate rich can be seen as the members of the social upper class in America, which is based on corporate wealth. While most of the contemporary controllers of corporations on the *Fortune* lists are members of high society, high society also includes widows of great wealth, retired tycoons, heiresses, and young people who are not yet directors of big corporations but have inside tracks to such positions. In other words, we need to supplement the view of the corporate rich derived purely from current corporate control positions with a view that captures the generational dynamics of the big business class. At this point the most useful approximate indicators of high society have been provided by Domhoff, who has shown that there is a cohesive upper class based on corporate wealth and who has provided several indices of membership in that class.[11]

The corporate rich may be viewed, then, as big corporate controllers plus high society. Controlling the means by which people live, doing so over time, and benefiting materially and mightily from that control, the corporate rich are the ruling class.

What, then, of politics? "Rule" is a political term, and politics has to do with authoritative decision-making in a society.

1. The most important class of authoritative decisions being those made or enforced with respect to the basic economic structure and distribution of benefits in a country, any class that dominates the economy, whether through the medium of corporations or through the medium of government control, already dominates the largest chunk of politics. Economic relations *are* political relations, too.

Most political scientists today deny that there is a ruling class. For them, the very concept is but a term in the obsolete vocabulary of ideologies of the left.[12] This denial is accomplished chiefly by reading economics out of politics—by treating business as some sphere of activity which, unlike government, is not political. But the dichotomy between economics and politics is, as we have seen, meaningless.

2. Of course, governmental *institutions* are not the same as corporate institutions, and it is necessary to examine the national state separately. The national state is democratic in form, even if democratic form does not extend to the politics of the economic world and even if the state is "intolerant of any serious oppo-

sition opinion that . . . [goes] beyond the general structure of capitalist institutions." [13] But, unfortunately for orthodox democratic mythology, it is easy to demonstrate that the corporate rich dominate the governmental system as well as the corporate system—though in the case of government, control is more informal and indirect and, possibly, more recent.

It is not certain when the current domination of the governmental system by the corporate rich began. Some social scientists saw the 1930's as a political decade, with some real balance of social forces in government (before the corporation man came to dominate administrative circles during World War II).[14] Others argue that the final "triumph of conservatism" against anticorporate challenges within government dates from World War I.[15] In any event, the corporate elite so dominate the governmental process today that no major state policy jeopardizes the corporate system from which they benefit.

Every major policy reveals in its actual provisions the objective of protecting the interests of the upper class. Since major policies set the framework within which lesser ones are formulated, minor policies are not incompatible with ruling class interests. In discussing the interests that policy serves, it is important to bear in mind that in general the interests of the majority of people in this society and of the majority of readers of this book are in conflict with those of the corporate rich—a situation that follows from the latter's domination of the economic process in which most of us are nonowning workers, whether of a plain or a fancy type.

The corporate rich are a political ruling class in the fullest sense, directly dominating economic institutions and indirectly dominating governmental ones.

Having defined the ruling class, it shall be our purpose in the remainder of this chapter to *demonstrate* the reality of its corporate power; to *analyze* the odd role of labor organizations in this society; to *demonstrate* that state policies do reflect ruling class interests; and to *explain* why, despite democratic forms, the state remains unavailable as an instrument of democratic self-governance.

THE REALITY OF CORPORATE POWER

That those who control the big corporations are in a position to exercise power over others is widely admitted by both liberal defenders and radical critics of our social order (while largely ignored by political scientists).[16] But it is important to realize that what power the economic elite have, others do *not* have, for corporate power is not the power of classical political theory, where decision-makers act as responsible agents of a self-governing people. Corporate power is irresponsible; it is the ability to make decisions that affect other people and that other people are effectively compelled to live with. Moreover, the *criterion* of corporate decision-making is long-term profits, not social need.

To some extent, big corporate power is exercised at the expense of other businesses. But in its most socially consequential form, monopolistic power means the powerlessness of the general working population. Consider, for example, the power to hire and fire people in accordance with the requirements for profit. The bigger the employer, the greater the number of people directly and indirectly affected by this power. As even workers with much seniority or with professional training learn in a recession, employees have no right either to get or keep a socially useful job, or indeed a job of any kind. Consider also the power of the corporation's managers to determine the production and sale of goods. This means the alienation from the production process of those who actually work to create the goods

—the lack of workers' control over their own labor or its fruits. Consider, further, the power of the oligopolies to administer prices to keep up with (and even ahead of) wage increases.[17] This means that the consumer is unable to get the affected goods at their actual value. Consider business investment, which shapes not only future production but the very ecology of urban, suburban, and rural life. The bigger the firm, the more far-reaching the effects of its investment policies. Investment, like all corporate power, responds to the call of profit, not of human needs. If it is more profitable to produce snowmobiles than to build adequate moderate-cost housing, then people are both inadequately housed and offended by intense sonic pollution.

Let us not fail to consider the most important corporate power of all—that of allocating personal income in wages, salaries, dividends, expense accounts, and so forth. Those who preside over the corporate world reap, in addition to intangible benefits, tremendous material benefits. The great fortunes of our time are rooted in the corporate world.[18] Economic inequality is systemic and persistent: the poorest 19 percent of the people received less than 5 percent of all income in 1963.[19] This was less than half a century earlier.[20] In 1969 the richest 5 percent of all U.S. families received more than twice as much of all income as did the entire poorest fifth of the families.[21] In the 1970 U.S. Census most families still received an annual income of less than $10,000.[22] Most people make, at best, enough to get by at the current mode of living (in which many machines once regarded as luxurious marvels—for example, telephones, cars, and refrigerators—are now expensive necessities). Many people make much less than is needed to live adequately at present. The affluent majority eludes us and will *continue* to elude us. The immediate reason is that not enough people have jobs that pay very well. If U.S. family income has gone up, most of the increase is accounted for by inflation and by the increased number of working women.[23] If real wages also increase, as they did before the 1970's, heightened medical costs and the disintegration of the larger family increase the prospect for abject poverty in old age.[24]

The smaller the segment at the top that is considered, however, the relatively richer it is (and the greater the proportion of its income derived from stock dividends).[25] The possession of wealth is even more unequally distributed than is annual income.[26] Complex tax legislation has given rise to complex means of minimizing income taxes and inheritance taxes; this makes it difficult to determine just how rich the richest people are. The richest people are, however, the corporate rich.[27]

American society may be affluent, but this term is more predictive of how our productive apparatus could be the basis for equitable and generalized economic security (under radically different social arrangements) than it is descriptive of the daily experience of the ordinary citizen in the economic struggle. At present the extreme affluence of a relatively very few is based on the real insecurity of the many. This inequality reflects the actual economic power of the corporate rich—the power to allocate income and, thus, wealth.

Though it is a system of real power—the power of some people over many others—there are no democratic pretensions (as yet) within the corporate world. The system is avowedly hierarchical. Liberal theory holds that in the final analysis power cannot be exercised over a person except by his actual consent; this is why thinkers who take liberalism seriously cannot find any justification for corporate power.[28] Nevertheless, it exists. It exists, moreover, because the state guarantees rather than limits corporate privileges. For corporate power "the safeguards . . . , both in law and in custom, are great."[29]

The corporate world is both a private and a public

system of power. It is private in that it is not even legitimized by the formal routine of republican responsibility. It is public in that it affects us all whether we like it or not.

THE ROLE OF "LABOR"

But aren't corporate powers limited by unions? So might inquire one of the many people who are unduly impressed by the union movement. In the early 1930's few were so impressed, as union membership dropped drastically. Rising unemployment made it easier to break unions, and the conservative leaders of the American Federation of Labor had little enthusiasm for "organizing the unorganized." Yet there were elements in national government which, working with the more liberal and far-seeing fringes of the business elite, correctly feared a continuing increase in "labor unrest." As Domhoff wrote in concluding his study of the Wagner Act of 1935, "by making certain concessions and institutionalizing their conflict with labor. . . [these members of the corporate rich and their coreformers] avoided the possibility of serious political opposition to the structure of the corporate system." [30] It was the Wagner Act that paved the legal way for the rise of mass industrial unionism.

The new industrial unions ultimately demonstrated the wisdom of the elite's gamble in channeling rather then repressing worker discontent. For soon the leaders of these unions were well-paid oligarchs who, once the initial organizing struggles had abated, purged their ranks of radicals. The leaders were and are explicitly committed to capitalism. They, too, lost their enthusiasm for organizing the unorganized, and union membership stagnated at a higher level, still far short of a majority of workers.

American unions are federated (not united) and rely

mainly on economic bargaining within the framework of any given industry. This collective bargaining process does not interfere with the corporate pricing freedom that erodes wage increases. The logic of this strategy, which is one of operating within the constraints of industrial capitalism, leads to a de facto dependence on the economic well-being of the corporations (and thus their controllers). Often the leaders' collaboration with corporate heads is quite explicit.[31]

The unions' strategy cannot end the economic insecurity and powerlessness of workers. Only a socialist strategy (of a democratic, not a statist, sort) could, if successful, accomplish that.* This is because insecurity and powerlessness are the necessary companions of economic control by capital. It is no wonder that there is no evidence that unions have had much effect on the *general* wage level in America.[32]

This is not to say that working-class struggles in America have been inconsequential. In fact, labor struggle has erupted repeatedly in our history, and the rise in strikes since the mid-1960's has been accompanied by an increase in spontaneous wildcat strikes (the result of rank-and-file discontent with union leaders' contract settlements). These struggles, legal as well as illegal, have certainly protected workers' wage and salary positions in some occupations, have prevented the firings of some workers, and in the most organized industries have resulted in some improvement in working conditions. Important improvements, yes. Basic changes, no. Workers are more and more dissatisfied with the equity and quality of work life in America, yet union leaders more and more find themselves containing (rather than advancing and developing) workers' struggles. Corporate executives informally rely on union leaders to sell contract settlements to members, an increasingly difficult task. When United

* See Chapter Six: The Excluded Alternative.

Automobile Workers head Walter P. Reuther died in
1970, the Chrysler Corporation vice-chairman, Virgil
Boyd, commented:

It's taken a strong man to keep the situation under control. I hope that whoever his successor may be he can exercise equal internal discipline.[33]

Union leaders evidence no basic dissatisfaction
with the order of things as they are. Thus, if these leaders were powerful in government it would mean labor
representation only in an essentially misleading sense.
But it is interesting to note that the managerial executives who head unions are not even in a very strong governmental position. The number of Congressmen responsive to union leadership is quite small compared
to the business-class bias of Congress as a whole, and
union representation in the more powerful executive
branch is virtually nonexistent. Only very occasionally
has even the Department of Labor been in the hands of
a union leader. The National Labor Relations Board
has not been in labor hands. The Department of Commerce, on the other hand, is ordinarily headed by a
businessman, and, in addition, is full of business advisory committees that afford corporate access to detailed government policy-making.[34]

The union movement thus has not put working people in a position to limit corporate power in any
substantial way. About the only constraint working
people impose on business is one which, in their role as
consumers, they can hardly avoid imposing. As with
any economy, capitalism must produce things that can
be marketed because people feel they need them.* Unwanted things cannot generally be sold; thus they pro-

* Even this "limit" is diminishing in importance as (1) corporate
expansion finds markets abroad; (2) government, mainly using taxes
coercively collected from people, buys unnecessary goods from
industries; and (3) corporate advertising exploits human weaknesses in order to create new needs in people.

duce no profits. Of course, it does not follow from this that people are able to get all they need, much less that they can feel confident that they will be able to meet their future needs for food, shelter, clothing, and medicine.

THE PATTERN OF GOVERNMENT POLICY

In modern society the state performs the function of maintaining the political system of economic organization. While the decision-making authority that captains of industry are in a position to exercise through their institutions—primarily corporations—is of enormous consequence to the people, it is itself secondary to and dependent on the state's authority. The laws passed by the national state do, in the American case, permit decisions about economic life to be made by a very few private individuals acting in their own interests. The democratic form of the government has little relevance when the bulk of the actually most important social decisions are made by other institutions entirely removed from popular control. Unfortunately, there is even more to the class power structure than that, for the important decisions over which the government does retain day-to-day control reflect the domination of the state by corporate interests.

Nowhere is the domination of the governmental process by the powers that be so clearly reflected as in national policy outputs. Not only does the structure of major policies reveal the objective of protecting ruling class interests but minor policies prove compatible with these interests as well.

Careful analysis of the actual content and consequences of government policies provides important evidence bearing on the question of "Who governs?" Michael Parenti has written of the tendency in American political science "to underplay or completely ignore policy outputs" and to omit "analysis of the actual effects of policies." [35] Contemporary political science prefers to focus on the array of groups and "political actors" having some say, however superficial, in policy-making. The tendencies toward trivia and apologia that are still central in U.S. political science are inevitable so long as most of its practitioners are willing to accept any conceptual framework as a guide to research save one, the automatic exclusion being the ruling class concept. But despite the relative paucity of useful research on policy, enough information is available from diverse sources for us to be able to take a brief look at some major and minor policies.

1. Economic Policy

Economic policy is, in terms of social consequences, the most important policy of the national state. The term "economic policy" is broad enough so that a great number of patterns of government action—even all of them—might be in some sense part of it. Let us first consider actions designed to affect the economic engine as a whole—actions designed to affect such aspects of the general state of the corporate economy as wages and employment, exports and imports, interest and prices, state spending and state taxes, and, of course, profits.

Besides the Presidency itself, the offices that bear on economic policy include the Council of Economic Advisers, the Federal Reserve Board, the Office of Management and Budget, and the Treasury Department, as well as other advisory and policy-making bodies. The President is clearly charged with the responsibility for ensuring the stability and continued growth of the corporate economy. The Presidential obligation to formulate policies for the existing capitalist economy was formalized in the Employment Act of 1946.

It is impossible for the government to formulate policies promoting the well-being of the economy as presently organized without protecting the corporate profits of the corporate rich. The economic system has its own dynamics: once corporate profits begin to stagnate (for whatever reason), investment begins to tumble, and collapse threatens. Stagnation of profits is inescapably linked with the much more neutral-sounding problems of inflation and recession, and was a concern necessarily central to the Nixon Administration's New Economic Policy of 1971. "We felt," said Treasury Secretary John Connally (a multimillionaire Democrat in the Republican Cabinet), "the profits of American business have not been all that big." [36]

The same point can be made somewhat differently by recalling that we have already shown that the economy as such is a radically unequal structure of power and wealth. When economic policy is designed to manage the existing economy by preventing its downturn through appropriate forms of state intervention, it must then objectively function to preserve the corporate wealth and power that are characteristic of that economy.[37] And, indeed, the actual effects of major general economic policies are demonstrably conservative of corporate wealth and power.

The most important fact about New Deal policy, for example, was that it rejected the socialist alternative and all of its economic aspects, from rationally planned economic development to the abolition of poverty and economic insecurity.[38] This was the automatic consequence of the aim of preserving the existing economy. It is true that many socioeconomic measures were then presented as helping the working people, but in the long run it was clear that this meant helping people by restoring the corporate economy. No policies antagonistic to the rejuvenation of the profit system of the corporate rich were implemented.[39]

The actual content of the Nixon Administration antirecession policies of 1971–1972 similarly benefited the ruling class. The substantial tax reductions for corporations (in the form of an investment credit), the surcharge on imports, and the auto excise tax repeal were examples of direct benefits. It was promptly pointed out that the whole package (which we have no space to discuss in detail here) was relatively inequitable to the working class.[40] Yet, the preexisting economy was *already* inequitable. Thus, the important thing about the New Economic Policy (or Nixonomics, as it was called) was not its particular inequities, but its basic purpose—namely, the rejuvenation of the existing economy without any departure from the substance of corporate prerogatives. This unavoidably meant benefiting the ruling class.

It is true that Nixon discussed full employment, as have all recent Presidents. But his Administration had previously encouraged increased unemployment and had chosen to discourage it only when it rose to economically dangerous heights.[41] Economic policy simply does not include the guarantee of jobs for people seeking work; such a legal guarantee was specifically rejected in the Employment Act of 1946.[42] Government jobs have been created only as a temporary expedient when unemployment threatened to create a social or economic crisis, as in the great depression of the 1930's. Economic policy consistently protects a free labor market in which unemployment, while fluctuating, persists at some level corresponding to the private needs of employers. For actual full employment would, *ceteris paribus,* give workers a mighty tool for attempting to increase their share of income, namely, a labor shortage. Keeping the economy growing on its present terms is the basic concern of economic policy, whereas a full employment policy would benefit workers more than the corporate rich.

In shaping economic policy, Congress operates

within the same constraints as the Administration.
Once accepting the capitalist assumption, as they invariably have, the committee chairmen who are the
power centers in Congress cannot formulate any program whose purpose is essentially different from the
President's. In practice, powerful Congressmen not
only defer to the Chief Executive but also insist that he
take action. Thus Congress in 1970 granted the President broad authority to stabilize prices, rents, wages,
and salaries. Under this virtual grant of law-making authority from Congress, President Nixon was able to
simply declare the 1971 wage and price freeze by fiat.
Congress made only marginal changes in the balance
of the antirecession program as it was submitted to
them for action.

2. Specific Economic Policies
Numerous minor policies can be seen as part of the
overall economic policy within whose framework they
operate. Such, for example, are the specific regulatory
policies toward different industries. The politics of regulation is one of the few policy areas to have received
moderately adequate critical attention from scholars.
As a result it has become clear to conservatives, liberals, and radicals alike that state regulation of corporations is generally protective of corporate power.[43] As
historian Gabriel Kolko has observed, "there has been
no sustained clash between any federal government
agency in existence or created during this century and
the industry it nominally regulates." [44] Major centers of
corporate power are protected by state policy choices
—if not through regulation, then through other privileges, or through inaction.[45]

But what of the most general regulatory policy of all
—antitrust? American antitrust policy makes corporate combinations in restraint of trade unenforceable
in the courts.[46] This means that the government has

opted for a noncartelization policy; that is, the state does not encourage the explicit grouping of U.S. industry into great rings and combines which formally regulate production, wages, and prices (although this was done temporarily during the New Deal).[47] This antitrust policy is a perfectly acceptable alternative for the corporate rich. Despite occasional prosecutions of violators, it does not prevent the monopolization of capitalism; it only regulates the form of the monopolization. If monopoly involves, in Milton Friedman's words, "sufficient control over a particular product or service to determine significantly the terms on which individuals shall have access to it," [48] there is no doubt that monopolistic power increasingly characterizes the corporate economy.

The 100 largest manufacturing corporations owned 38 percent of all assets in manufacturing in 1950; antitrust notwithstanding, the top 100 corporations owned 48 percent by 1970.[49] Reporting on his recent study of corporate size, profits, and taxes, Charles Vanik stated:

The share of total corporate profits of firms with assets over $1 billion has nearly doubled since 1959—from 28.4 percent of all profits in that year to 54.6 percent in 1971. In 1971, almost 55 percent of all corporate profits in America was achieved by the billion-dollar corporations, only 260 corporations in number.[50]

It is thus generally admitted of antitrust that, as one liberal scholar concluded, "no thoroughgoing application of it is likely or even possible." [51] This is *because* the government is fundamentally loath to intervene in the corporate world in any way antagonistic to big corporate interests. Of course, in a particular case corporate lobbying may, as a supplementary influence, help ward off threatened antitrust action. Thus it became known in 1972 that the giant International Telephone

and Telegraph Corporation had made between $200,-
000 and $400,000 available to finance the Republican
National Convention—after which the Justice Department settled its antitrust case with ITT out of court and
on favorable terms that permitted the company to
merge with the big Hartford Fire Insurance Company.[52]
The ITT case illustrates several things. One is the con-
tinual flow of corporate money into political finance.*
Another is the pervasiveness of corporate lobbying; although political scientists like to celebrate the great
number of groups that lobby, the fact is that most of the
groups active in Washington are businesses or business associations.[53] But the most important fact about
the ITT case is that, irrespective of the role the ITT con-
vention-underwriting offer played, the settlement was
perfectly ordinary and entirely precedented, of a piece
with corporate regulation generally. It was characteristic of the basic long-run politics of economic policy,
which is profoundly procorporate.

3. Domestic Social Policies

Numerous minor policies appear, at first glance, to be
less closely related to the economic policy framework.
But these policies, sometimes called welfare state policies, are in practice no different from antitrust policy.
They are not incompatible with ruling class interests.

There is, for example, a complex federal housing
program that has evolved over the last 35 years. It has
always been justified in terms of ameliorating the en-
demic shortage of decent modest-cost housing. The
most important component of the policy is government
insurance for private bank mortgages, which spurred
much private single-family home building for white
families able to afford new houses after World War II.[54]
Another component is public housing—that is, housing built by private contractors paid with funds trans-

* See Chapter Four: The Corporate Input.

ferred from Washington to local governments and then operated by cities almost entirely out of rents charged to moderately poor families. This housing has always represented a tiny fraction of all U.S. housing and a fraction of the adequate housing generally admitted to be needed (and public housing is itself a pale shadow of what it could be) [55]; for U.S. housing policy has, quite characteristically, been developed within the capitalist economic framework. This means that the government does not (1) redistribute income or (2) create jobs, so that all can afford decent housing; nor does it (3) enter the housing market to any large degree. This is not to say that the market is a "pure" private one, for government subsidies, direct and indirect, are extremely important to the private interests that cluster around metropolitan housing in America —banks, builders, real estate dealers, landlords, merchants, etc.

Another program of housing policy, urban renewal, was explicitly structured for maximum reliance on "private enterprise" and has not failed—except, quite inevitably, in its stated goal of providing "a decent home and a suitable living environment for every American family." [56] The search for profit, as Jeanne Lowe has written, "has not proved to be a reliable mechanism for generating adequate housing." [57] It is hard to understate the failure of urban renewal as a housing policy, for it has led to more destruction than construction, and such construction as has occurred has been at higher rent levels than the preexisting housing. In response to protest and criticism, urban renewal was expanded into a complex program whose sophisticated apparatus continued to fail. This is not to report that business interests in urban downtowns have not benefited from urban renewal, whose monies are increasingly turned to direct commercial use; it is to report that such new departures as subsidizing interest payments to banks on behalf of selected urban low-income families in fact placed money not in the people's hands but in the hands of businessmen, as in the not atypical Detroit case:

The policies in Detroit of the Federal Housing Authority, which is part of H.U.D., have turned into a major scandal that could cost the Government $100 million and possibly much more.

Under the guise of programs to help the poor buy their own homes, thousands of welfare residents were pushed into old or dilapidated dwellings. Real estate speculators roamed old neighborhoods buying up houses for a few thousand dollars each, getting them appraised by F.H.A. appraisers at double, triple or quadruple the purchase prices, then selling them to the poor, including thousands of welfare recipients who could not keep them up.

To date about 6,500 homes under these programs have been foreclosed in Detroit, and 750 to 1,000 more are foreclosed every month. The total could surpass 20,000, about 7 or 8 per cent of the homes in the city. The abandoned houses, in turn, help to blight entire blocks and neighborhoods.[58]

Despite the complete failure of urban renewal as a social welfare policy, the latest innovation in housing policy, Operation Breakthrough, is but a subsidy to capitalists, in this case in the area of prefabricated industrial housing.[59]

Housing policy is not unique—it is typical. Domestic social policies may not, in many cases, directly benefit the corporate rich as a whole. But they never poach on the opportunities for profitable private investment in any economic field. If they did, these policies might be antagonistic to the present or future interests of the corporate world.

For rural America the farm program is, incredibly, still defended as a means of preserving the family farm.[60] But big farmer commodity interests are personally and politically represented in the Department of Agriculture.[61] The farm program is so structured that the bigger owners, who are big indeed, actually get relatively more money than do small operators.[62] The farm program is but a business subsidy. Could farm policies be antagonistic to elite interests? Yes, if they removed farmland from the private marketplace and implemented a land reform policy (as badly needed here as in many "underdeveloped" countries) designed to redistribute land or to encourage development of cooperative and collective forms of farming. This would restrict the agricultural sector as a possible field for corporate profits. It would limit corporate freedom and future expansion, curbing the growth of agribusiness. It would also be quite incompatible with economic policy, and is not contemplated in Washington.

All domestic policies are so structured as to be nonantagonistic to the free enterprise system that is vital to the business class and to the elite tycoons. This is true irrespective of the type of policy. It is true of military procurement policy.[63] It is true of national medical insurance.[64] It is even—perhaps especially—true of welfare itself, whose minimal and demeaning payments are a substitute for any such policy as income redistribution, job creation, housing construction, etc., and have historically been designed to be noncompetitive with local labor wage rates.[65] Literally never incompatible with corporate interests, minor policies are often incompatible with noncorporate interests—weapons systems (with their cost overruns) versus the ordinary taxpayer, the farm program versus the small farmer, urban renewal versus the urban renter, social welfare versus the poor, and so on.

Minor policies are ordinarily justified in terms of broad public goals whose appeal tends to obscure the actual content of policy. The actual policies of the state (not their idealizations and rationalizations) do not, in practice, advance the social goals so prominent in the language of contemporary school textbooks, governmental legislation, and party politics. The reason is not bureaucratic rigidity, for no one is so flexible and politically accessible as the American bureaucrat; rather, it is the very structure of policy, formulated as it is in the framework of a fundamentally procorporate economic policy.

Foreign Policy

Like economic policy, foreign policy is a major policy. Unlike many minor policy formation processes, foreign policy alternatives are, by and large, actively formulated and executed by the corporate rich.[66] It is no very great task to determine whether the rich make policy in their own interest, for much recent critical work by historians demonstrates clearly the actual content and impact of American foreign policy.

U.S. foreign policy is a historically continuous expression of a specific imperialism designed to produce American domination of as much of the world as possible. The work of William Appleman Williams, in particular, has been extremely important in demonstrating that the continuity in U.S. foreign policy traces back at least as far as the days of the formulation of the Open Door policy at the end of the last century.[67] There is debate, of course, over what the search for domination means. To the obvious implications of the fact that American business interests are aggressively expanding overseas under the generally supportive aegis of governmental diplomatic, political, and military interventions there are several objections: that liberal idealism is actually the motive of the policy-makers; that the costliness of the Vietnam war proves the irrelevance thereto of economic motivations; that the Pentagon really is manipulating the President. These objections are possible only because two questions have not been asked: Does American foreign policy benefit the ruling class? Does it benefit the ruled classes?

The foreign policy made by the uppermost class does benefit its makers. When successful, as it often has been, American imperialism secures a political space in which corporate profits can be made by investment in low-wage countries, by protection of overseas resources from competitive exploitation, by sales to overseas customers (including governments), and by other means.[68]

Military force, open and secret, actual and threatened, has often been needed to protect from insurgency the type of local government the U.S. government has wanted.[69] And in the formulation of U.S. counterrevolutionary imperialism, there is no evidence that military men were behind the scenes when Presidents developed their policies for protection of the so-called free world.

In this century, the United States has opposed liberal revolutions, socialist revolutions, and communist coups alike. Political structures and forces are, therefore, the dependent variables of U.S. foreign policy. The anticommunist ideology of freedom and democratic self-determination (whether or not sincerely held by this or that policy-maker) is not the long-run source of American conduct; indeed, liberalism has usually been a casualty of U.S. overseas intervention. Which political forces will be opposed, which political structures supported, varies from place to place and time to time. Of course, broadly speaking, it is true that the forces of the left have been the general enemy of the century, even (perhaps especially) in World War II.[70] Why? Because what is indeed invariable in U.S. foreign policy is the intended protection of American economic interests. Protection of opportunities for the business system as a whole has always been built into U.S. foreign policy.[71] The Marshall Plan in Europe was no exception.[72] The Alliance for Progress was no exception.[73] Now, members of the ruling class see a promising era of economic development under private enterprise in Southeast Asia when the war against the Vietnamese revolution has ended.[74] In the long run, U.S. investment in underdeveloped states retards independent economic development.[75] U.S. policy invariably encourages overseas investment; foreign aid is no exception whatever.[76] Many know these things well and still reject an "economic determinism" explanation of American overseas policy. Such a catchphrase simply signifies a refusal to confront the fact that U.S. foreign policies, whatever else they are intended to do, are invariably designed to benefit the ruling class. Insofar as the forces of the left appear to threaten to foreclose general opportunity for the U.S. corporate system, as they frequently do, they are opposed; "the fight against communism helps the search for profits." [77]

American foreign policy does not benefit ordinary Americans.[78] Unlike ruling classes of old, the American elite do not send their promising young men into the front lines. Largely working class infantry face the greatest dangers, while foreign civilians bear the brunt of the firepower. If it is terribly obvious that the people of the underdeveloped world suffer from U.S. foreign policy—from genocide in Vietnam, to embargo in Cuba, to support for poverty-perpetuating elites everywhere—it is nevertheless often said that at least war orders help our own people; a war economy at least provides jobs. This benefit is illusory for four reasons. First, additional jobs are not easy to measure positively against losses of thousands of young men, and against the social costs of war. Second, the periodic wars that are inherent in the imperial policy now cause rising taxes and prices that are the immediate (but not fundamental) cause of a higher cost of living. Third, corporations that increasingly exploit low-paid labor overseas (a process impossible without an interventionist foreign policy) simply increase profits at the expense of domestic workers. Fourth and most fundamentally, the arms-making jobs are within the framework of capitalism, and they cannot help the worker escape the alienation, powerlessness, and economic insecurity of his work life, for these things are built into "defense" jobs just as they are into virtually all jobs in a capitalist system. American foreign policy, no matter how militaristic and aggressive, cannot end the economic insecurity and alienated powerlessness of the metropolitan majority. The people understand, generally, how little they benefit from war. That is why to prepare the people for war, government must engage in massive propaganda efforts to project threats to popular well-being even greater than war itself. Genuine democracy is incompatible with an imperial policy, since the latter calls for sacrifices from many and benefits for few.

BEHIND THE DEMOCRATIC FAÇADE

In the economic realm, the corporate rich rule officially and directly. In the governmental realm they do not rule officially. But they so dominate the governmental process that major policies redound to their benefit—and lesser ones are compatible with their interests—even though the interests of the majority of the people differ from those of the elite. Even a brief review of aspects of governmental policy reveals the essential reality of corporate political power. If policy output analysis is insufficient to reveal the complex mechanisms of domination, it does show that the economic ruling class is also an effective governmental ruling class.

In regard to government, class rule is not a matter of a hidden conspiracy—even though the clouds of ideology obscure it—but rather a matter of the political logic of a policy-making process effectively dominated by the corporate rich. Government policies interrelate to form a web of mutually supportive patterns of state action. The web of capitalist state policy can incorporate some specific interests and exclude others, but it is fundamentally predicated upon the primacy of the existing economic power structure and cannot avoid protecting corporate interests against challenges, actual or potential.

What the elite require in order to *continue* to effectively dominate the governmental process is a set of state authorities whose policy-making is carried out in the framework of the capitalist economy. Government policy will then continue to protect the system of private power that is the corporate world (to the benefit of its controllers). Moreover, since there is no important policy unaffected by society's economic structure, the corporate framework will impose its logic on policy generally; policy will bear the inescapable imprint of the capitalist assumption.

What is involved, then, is not so much control of the governmental offices by a businessmen's clique or through a capitalist plot as it is the continued protection of the corporate system by policy-makers. Such protection will mean that the distinctive interests of the big business class are invariably protected in politics. Indeed, these interests are presupposed as the basis on which alternatives are debated, while other classes and groups must compromise in the pull and tug of interest group politics—if indeed they have any influence at all. In terms of the national state, class rule is a question not of secret dictatorship but of actual power in the visible government.

It is a matter of interest (but of secondary import) that the uppermost class is rather well represented in office—and in the key executive posts, better represented than any other occupational group. Thus, in

1956, Mills found that most of the occupants of the 50 key Administration posts were the "legal, managerial and financial members of the corporate rich." [79] And in 1967, Domhoff found that over two-thirds of the heads of the key departments of War and Defense, Treasury, and State from 1932 on had been members of the social upper class based on the corporate rich.[80] These and other data support Douglass Cater's observation that "a recognizable group of skilled operatives shuttles back and forth between private enterprise and the key posts of foreign policy, defense and finance." [81]

The top executive authorities—"the Administration"—constitute only part of the governmental system. There are also Senators, Representatives, judges, career bureaucrats with influence, military leaders, and subnational leaders; and if their role in decision-making is of second-order importance, it is nevertheless real. The direct office-holding of the ruling class is concentrated at the executive top. But the business class as a whole predominates in other decision-making offices. For example, a study by Donald R. Matthews dealt with the occupational backgrounds of both incumbents and their fathers concluded that "the narrow base from which decision-makers appear to be recruited is clear." [82] He added:

> [*Our*] *decision-makers, taken as a broad whole, are very far from being a cross-section of the electorate. Rather there seems to be a sort of class ranking of political offices in the United States—the more important the office, the higher the social status of the normal incumbent.*[83]

Matthews had no background data on the military hierarchy and the Supreme Court, but other studies verify the preponderance of business-class backgrounds there.[84] As to Congress, recent data not only confirm Matthews' findings but also show that a large majority of incumbents admit to maintaining outside business interests while in office.[85]

Important as it is to realize what the economic backgrounds of the office-holding elite actually are, what the ruling class requires as the sine qua non of its power is not monopolization of key offices but the maintenance of a national government continuously committed to corporate capitalism by the very character of its agencies and policies. Since we very evidently have such a government, the question then becomes: How can it be maintained?

One way this government can maintain itself is by repressing subversive attempts to challenge existing economy and government *outside* the channels of the electoral process. The character of the electoral process then becomes vital. For the business elite to continue as the ruling class, the electoral process must operate so as to exclude from power people embodying or responsive to interests that are antagonistic to the interests of the corporate rich. Given the ideology of all major parties and interest groups, which are unshakably committed to "free enterprise," and given the character of the political culture in which they operate, which is decreasingly but importantly procapitalist in ideology, this control over political recruitment is not difficult to perpetuate. As long as the semiofficial major parties manage to maintain their dominant positions in the electoral process, they automatically serve ruling class interests by their commitment to the corporate economic framework as a basis for policy. Yet the domination of the electoral process by the current constellation of political organizations is not merely a matter of their momentum, for any status quo must be maintained against challenges, actual and potential. And several important forces do indeed operate to protect the capitalist purity of the electoral process.

1. The financing of elections is an important conservative safeguarding force. Elections in America are cheap when compared to corporate profits or government budgets. They are incredibly expensive when

compared to the income of even a moderately well-paid professional. As subsequent chapters will point out, offices of consequence are the most expensive ones for which to campaign. Most of the money raised for national campaigns comes from big contributors. The financing of elections for major offices is, in fact, an important aspect of the politics of the corporate rich.* The most significant impact of election financing is on the attitudes of the office-seeker; he or she knows that for any position of consequence it is necessary to get funds from business-class supporters.** Anticorporate attitudes will not often be compatible with this requirement.

2. Were there an insurgent anticorporate party of consequence in America, it would find winning control of "the government" through the electoral process next to impossible because of the incredible diffusion of decision-making authority in the system. The sharing of policy-making authority among many formal branches and levels of government is carried to a greater length in the United States than in any other major nation. Besides the policy-making Presidency there are two policy-making national legislatures, a policy-making federal court system, and innumerable policy-making boards, commissions, agencies, and public corporations—not to mention military leaders and state governments. "Separation of powers" was originally defended, nearly two centuries ago, as a protection against conquest of government by a radical majority.[86] It will serve that function today when an insurgent movement tries to seek power through the murky U.S. electoral process, for none of the authorities is at present ideologically neutral, and each is in a position to check the official acts of others. As for to-

* See Chapter Three: Financing National Elections.
** See Chapter Five: The Excluded Alternative.

day's voting public, it is quite impossible for it to learn very much about, let alone control, so complex and fragmented a decision-making process.

3. The power of corporations, and employers generally, to hire and fire is seldom recognized as the means of political control that it is. In terms of rewards, a political career is an exceedingly common route to a good executive business post, and the implications of this fact cannot escape the career-oriented politician (be he legislator, administrator, military officer, or the like). Of course, within organizations, including non-corporate institutions, there are norms with political content. To be advanced to higher offices that are understood to entail certain types of responsibilities, the employee has to be seen by his superiors as reliable. A person deeply disturbed about corporate power, say to the point of action, cannot expect to be considered "responsible." (Organizational norms are not neutral, and they seldom reward the maverick. Indeed, in terms of punishments, employers are on the whole quite free to fire dissidents in their employ.) Yet, as Milton Friedman has put it, "In order for men to advocate anything they must in the first place be able to earn a living." [87] The employee who engages in radical political advocacy and action, in or out of the workplace, ordinarily does risk his or her own job. That is why serious radical movements will gradually come to understand the vital need to fight against political firings as part of any larger struggle against corporate power.

4. Politics involves the struggle for control of the minds of people. Indeed, there is no political rule without some minimum willingness of an effective majority of people to obey authority (whether they like it or not). As important as armed force is in political rule, in the final analysis its effectiveness is determined by people's decisions to resist or to obey. Consequently, "persuasion" and "manipulation" (of opinion) have

been defined as forms of political power.[88] And, in our society, ideological control of the means of shaping opinion constitutes an important conservative political force.

Many are the social institutions that aid in the socialization of members or other audiences into the capitalist political culture. These include youth clubs, religious institutions, labor unions and professional societies, schools, civic and voluntary associations, political parties, the army, and the mass media. In some cases institutional influence on political socialization is direct; in others it is indirect. But in all these cases it is real. It is not only in the sociologist's totalitarian dictatorship that nongovernmental institutions are integrated into the service of the powers that be; this occurs informally in our own totalitarian democracy. The reader who has followed us this far can supply examples from his or her own experience as Girl Scout, student, soldier, professional-society member, etc. We shall single out for brief examination one of these institutions: the mass media.

Twentieth-century politicians wisely place tremendous importance upon communications and propaganda by mass media, for to the extent that people are influenced by what they see and read and hear, the media define political reality. Our media are free. This means, primarily, that we have little state censorship. Books like this are published; dissent is expressed.

However, tokenism is not a phenomenon limited to race relations. For the dissent which this book constitutes is, indeed, an exception that proves the rule. What is the rule? That the media are means of power at the disposal of holders of power.

With few exceptions, the business class owns the media. Those among the media which—like Time Inc. —are among the largest corporations are controlled by members of the corporate rich. Corporate advertising is essential at the level of nation-wide communication by publication or broadcast, for the media are profit-making corporations deriving their main income from ads. Common economic interests unite those who control the biggest media with the rest of the corporate rich. (Similarly, broader common interests unite the controllers of the lesser media with the business class of which *they* are a part.)

Government policy permits the communications industry substantial leeway in operating the media. In broadcasting, unlike publishing, there is a central regulating agency, and Federal Communications Commission regulation is like industrial regulation generally—it confers the benefits of stability and moderated competition while allowing the industry substantial leeway to make decisions in its own interests.[89] Since these interests include those shared with the corporate rich, the entire ruling class is in a position to benefit from the media. That they actually do so benefit can be seen in considering the actual communications content of the media.

Corporate executives do not have to dictate every detail of content in order for reporters to understand that they have no freedom to describe reality just as they see it.[90] The very job of reporters, photographers, columnists, and script writers is to file observations with editors and producers. Editors and producers report to publishers and to senior executives who, in turn, report to the corporate controllers. The structure of the media is quite as hierarchical as that of other corporations; this structure contains the process of deciding what information is presented and, perhaps more importantly, how it is presented. That media content benefits the ruling class can be demonstrated through a brief review of some reformist criticisms of the media —criticisms that we think miss the mark.

1. Advertiser pressure: Critics note that an adver-

tiser can withdraw his business from a medium in response to content unfavorable to his particular industry; that in terms of the advertisements themselves, no type of lie (from the simplest to the psychosexually most subtle) is too great for the ad industry; and that the media serve the function of generating consumer demand through the creation of false needs.

We have no objection to these criticisms. Yet they omit the fact that advertisers are not interested only in the sale of goods but, like the media owners, have a clear economic interest in ideological combat. Virtually all media fare—news, columns, and shows as well as the ads themselves—must have some ideological content of one or another type; and the prevailing ideology of American opinion-shaping institutions, media included, is overwhelmingly procapitalist.

The troubles of our people are never traced to the corporate capitalist system as such. Thus, if the economic cause of poverty has anything to do with the power of employers to pay wages inadequate for sustenance, and to fire workers to protect profits, one would never know it from broadcast and published news. These sources merely recount unemployment and welfare data, while systematically singling out riots and strikes as the principal willful actions that have deleterious economic effects. More precisely stated, the prevailing ideology denies the existence of a ruling class. The concept of "ruling class," or even of "corporate rich," is virtually alien to the mass media. This means that radical criticism of the corporate rich and their control of economy and state is absent. Criticisms of "the War," "the Administration," and "the Pentagon" abound (and these may even occasionally be correct criticisms), but the most elementary facts about the top of the U.S. social structure are excluded from the media as thoroughly in the 1970's as they were in the 1960's and 1950's.

2. Television violence: Critics note that TV violence is pervasive and inescapable, and they ask what effects this has on viewers (especially children). They criticize the government's appointment of a violence study panel because the three major networks were given the prerogative of vetoing panel appointments (an act perfectly characteristic of communications policy). [91] They point to the subsequent protest by research team members that the official 1972 report (based on their research but drawn up by the panel) seriously understated the actual effects uncovered.[92]

Again, we have no objection to these criticisms. But the main social significance of TV violence is not its triggering of an observable violent action by a child (as serious an effect as that is). Consider, rather, the ideological front. Violence is but part of the generalized portrait of people as inhuman to people (people are weak, selfish). The idea that people are essentially competitive with and disrespectful of others is conveyed just as much through the undermining "humor" of the comedy show as through the violence of the western. The law, on the other hand, stands as an impartial refuge protecting people from the bestiality of their fellows. The theory implicit in the content is quite elementary and quite Hobbesian, and it serves the interests of power well.

It matters little whether cynicism about human nature is spread as a matter of calculation, as a reflex prejudice of the decision-makers, or as a pandering to the perceived attitudes of the audience. The point is that the portrait is wrong. Consider working-class struggle one of the types of experience omitted. The TV "worker" is the ineffectual type (Chester Riley, Ralph Norton) who never struggles in unison with his fellows. Instead of Archie Bunker as a harmless (?) racist, how about Archie Bunker as uniting with other workers (black and white) in a Brooklyn postal union local to trigger an illegal national rank and file mailmen's walkout—and winning a wage boost from the government, as happened in 1970? Of course, this is asking too much from the media. This is precisely the point. Vital aspects of reality needed to portray people as they really are are absent, and perhaps the most serious omission is that of people struggling together against a common oppression.

3. News management: Critics note that government secrets are unavailable to the media and people; that government now provides most of the national "news" to the reporting staffs of the media; [93] and that the Freedom of Information Act has not really opened up the bureaucracy to the media.[94]

Once again, we have no objection to these criticisms. But the most consequential news management is that done by the media itself of the rather substantial amount of available information. For example, consider the electoral process ("democracy"). The media take the clash of parties and politicians quite seriously. Their coverage and interpretations generate interest in electoral politics and, more importantly, suggest their democratic validity. National Presidential nominating conventions are treated as extremely consequential events (perhaps they are, but not because it makes much *political difference* which of the serious contestants is nominated or later elected).

The prevailing ideology of the electoral process is that people should work for change within a framework that must ("realistically") accept the capitalist ("free enterprise") system. This ideology also proposes the invalidity (immorality and/or impracticality) of struggle that is not within the system. The repeated articulation of such ideas serves, of course, to create the very realities to which the ideology so eagerly points.

The media propagate this ideology, giving great play to such dissidents as Ralph Nader and Eugene

McCarthy who, whatever their virtues as exposers of real evils, have as an admitted purpose the channeling of discontent into the existing electoral process—to prove, as McCarthy so often said in his 1968 antiwar campaign, that the system works. Promotion of the ideology is in part an automatic consequence of giving great uncritical coverage to the major participants of the political game, and it is the most consequential news management of all.

Far be it from the media to expose the fraudulence of the competition between two virtually official parties with the same *basic* ideology. Far be it from the media to expose the common condition of the majority, for, as Mills wrote:

they do not articulate for the viewer or listener the broader sources of his private tensions and anxieties, his inarticulate resentments and half-formed hopes.[95]

Far be it from the media to demonstrate the meaning of Marcuse's formulation:

Free election of the masters does not abolish the masters or the slaves.[96]

For the media are but one of several opinion-shaping institutions that protect the capitalist assumption underlying the electoral process. This process ("democracy"), once in fact closed as a means of representing interests antagonistic to those of the corporate rich, is transformed from a potentially disruptive force into an actually conservative one, essential to class rule in America. If armed force is the stick of the American power structure, the electoral process is the indispensable carrot.

SUMMARY

Several forces transform the electoral process from a potential threat to corporate power into a mechanism

guaranteeing that policy-making incumbents are responsive to the interests of the elite. Beyond the mere
momentum of established law, custom, political parties, and interest groups, these several forces include
such elements as the fragmentation of official authority
(rendering republican responsibility impossible), employers' political power to fire and promote (in accordance with corporate politicoeconomic interests), and
the ideological role (on behalf of the existing order)
of such opinion-shaping institutions as the mass media.

The one of these conservative forces that we have
selected for further examination is election financing.
Though many people contribute to campaigns, financing is heavily dependent on the big contributors and
constitutes but one more obstacle to office-holding by
persons who are not of or for the elite. The greatest impact of election financing is on the attitudes of would-
be candidates, who understand how necessary it is to
get early money to start up their campaigns; under present circumstances private wealth is the source of this
early money. The big givers do not back those who
might threaten the system. Campaign financing reinforces the system, as we intend to show.

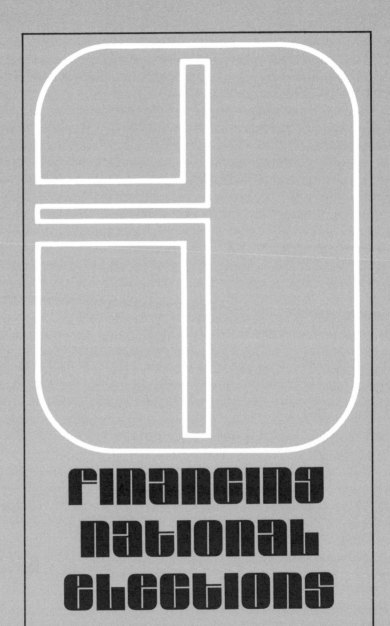

financing
national
elections

THE SIGNIFICANCE OF THE BIG GIVERS

Most national campaign cash comes from the big contributors. But the importance of the big givers does not derive from their providing any specific fraction of total election money. Rather, the importance of the fat cats of election finance derives from the fact that they are courted by all factions of both major parties irrespective of how much money is also being raised from mail drives, telethons, and other small-collection efforts.

The role of the rich in political finance springs not only from the needs of candidates for assistance, but also from the willingness of candidates to limit their political positions so that at the very least they pose no danger to the corporate power structure. In short, money is not given to those who threaten the system.

The most critical aspect of participation by big givers lies in their providing the early money needed by one who is not an incumbent and who is starting up a campaign to attain office for the first time. Unless the nonincumbent is personally rich, private wealth must be secured to get a campaign for any major office organized and begun.

In America, political party officials are usually unable to select the person who will run for election under the party label. Instead, candidates struggle to win the primary election or convention nominations of their respective parties. It is the money that is available for primary and preconvention campaigns that determines access to the nomination of one or another party. "Here," as election finance student Alexander Heard once put it, "persons with access to money find their greatest opportunity to influence the selection of public officials." [1]

Politicians understand the requirement for early money. Former U.S. Senator Fred R. Harris has written of the basic requirement of getting big contributors in the initial stages of a campaign. "I spent a great deal of personal time soliciting big contributors," Harris said of his 1964 Senatorial primary campaign; "the crucial financial stage was the successful solicitation of a few first big contributors." [2] *

It is the early money that goes to liberals, particularly to Democrats, which is most important in helping to prevent the articulation of an alternative left politics within the electoral process. The idea of having economic power and its benefits widely shared instead of undemocratically concentrated is an essentially leftist idea, and it is therefore the funding of any leftish candidates who might be inclined to articulate opposition to the corporate power structure and its domination of politics that is of most consequence for the stability of the system. The idea of a just and democratic social order simply has never been advocated from the right, while the left—for all its obvious political faults—has tended to stand for such an alternative. And, for a couple of generations, liberal Democrats have "dominate[d] the left alternative in this country, and the sophisticated rich want to keep it that way." [3]

While the most crucial impact of big money is at the early stages of liberal candidacies, the money given by the rich is not politically equal to similar amounts gotten from many small givers at any stage of any campaign. As election finance expert David Adamany has explained:

The large contributor has noteworthy advantages in exercising his influence within the political system. He is generally solicited for funds by someone close to the candidate or officeholder . . . and he is thus recognized at the center of power as having given vital assistance. A group of small

* This candid admission comes from a man who characterizes himself as a populist and who has boasted that most of the money he got in his 1964 campaign came from small gifts. For more on Fred Harris, see Chapter Six: The Excluded Alternative.

contributors . . . , even though they may give in the aggregate the same amount, are likely to be solicited by lesser persons who are farther from those who hold ultimate decision-making authority.[4]

Some of the big givers of politics are labor union officials whose contribution money is derived largely from collections from union members. Union leaders do not, however, supply such amounts of money as implied in equations like "big business and big labor"; they give much less than do businessmen, and, furthermore, their contributions do not undermine the business system and its class power structure.*

The big contributors represent for the most part the ruling class quietly funding the electoral process. Before assessing their role in more detail, however, we must review the nuts and bolts of campaign funding—how much elections cost, what campaign money is spent for, and how the money is raised. Our focus will be on the national level, particularly the Presidency.

UNCOVERING THE COST OF CAMPAIGNS

Information about who pays how much for political campaigns is vital to the question of what interests are actually being represented in the governmental process. Despite this, and perhaps on account of it, politicians have been quite reluctant to disclose the dynamics of their finances unless required to. A few politicians have made a point of disclosing fully their election finances (and such allied information as personal income and worth), but spontaneous voluntary disclosure has not yielded much information over the years. Federal laws, while they have never produced literally full disclosure, have brought forth a certain

---

* On the significance of union political spending see Chapter Five: Financing Liberalism.

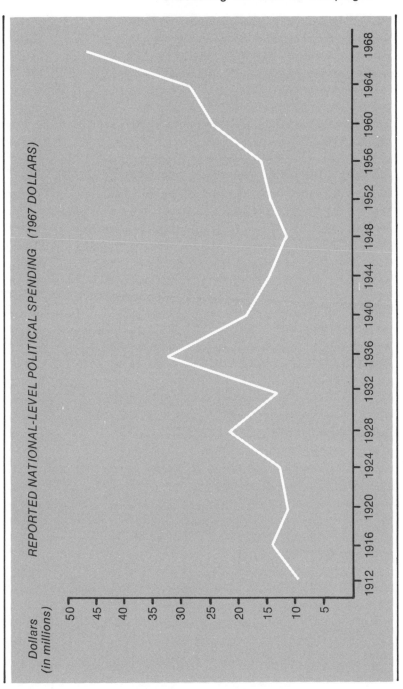

amount of information. At the state level, reporting laws vary from the fairly complete to the nonexistent.[5]

Some sort of financial reporting requirement for national-level political committees (those not operating entirely within one state) has been on the U.S. statute books since 1912, when the reported spending of Democratic, Republican, and Progressive committees totaled $2.9 million.[6] By 1968 these expenditures were reported as totaling $48.1 million.[7] The expenditures of national committees as reported under federal law are mapped for Presidential election years in Chart I.[8] Since the figures used for the chart are expressed in terms of constant 1967 dollars, the indicated increases are not artifacts of price inflation.

Since 1912, the records for national-level committees have usually shown Republican committees spending more than Democratic committees (and since 1936, more than Democratic plus labor committees). In 1968, Republican committees accounted for 55 percent of the spending, and in addition these committees transferred over twice as much money to state and local committees as national Democratic committees transferred to subnational units. Democratic committees accounted for 25 percent of the reported spending and labor union committees, spending on behalf of Democrats, for 4 percent, while the George Wallace campaign spent 16 percent of the total.[9] In 1972, Republican spending was again far ahead. In 1960, however, Democratic and labor committees together managed to outspend Republican committees nationally.

The numbers reflected in Chart I are based on data supplied by political committees in accordance with the law but not audited independently. They should not be taken as accurate totals, but as partial indicators of magnitudes and trends. Their utility for even this purpose diminished after 1936. A drop in reported national-level spending from $14.1 million in 1936 to $7.8 million in 1940 was a result of the passage of the Hatch Act of 1940, which limited individual contributions to one political committee to $5,000 and limited total political committee spending to $3 million per year. The parties then simply decentralized financing to state and local committees to mitigate the effects of the law.[10] The amount of money which was actually nationally oriented but derived from subnational (and nonreporting) committees thereby increased dramatically as reported spending dropped. In addition, the device of founding many theoretically separate national committees came to provide another method for circumventing the law, particularly useful in getting gifts totaling more than the $5,000 individual "limit."

Where they provided reasonably accurate information, state laws highlighted the limits of federal reporting laws of the pre-1972 period. Congressional candidates are subject to state reporting laws. David Rosenbloom has pointed out that for 34 U.S. Senate races of 1968, the grand total reported to Congress in accordance with federal disclosure law was $2.7 million, while the Senatorial primary and general election costs in California alone in that year were, according to reports filed in accordance with that state's laws, over $4 million.[11] In 1970 there was, for the first time, a national survey of Congressional campaign costs, according to which a verified total of $72 million (and an estimated total of $90 million) was spent; but only $13 million was reported to Congress in accordance with federal law.[12]

One of the means by which any law, state or federal, can be evaded is through the use of cash gifts which, unlike checks, leave no bank records. In 1967 Senate hearings, the Under Secretary of the Treasury, himself a former elected official, stated:

I am sure we are all aware that a large portion of election expenses are paid in cash. They don't appear any place.

There are strict provisions in most States that you must report cash. Nobody does.[13]

Between 1925 and 1972, primary and preconvention campaign expenses were explicitly excluded from reporting requirements. Between exemptions, loopholes, and the tradition of nonenforcement, federal law before 1972 failed to produce an accounting of the sources and uses of most national political money.

New provisions governing the disclosure of campaign fund sources and uses, signed into law in 1971, became legally effective in 1972. Any candidate for federal office, or any political committee that spends over $1,000 a year and supports such a candidate, must account for all expenditure items of more than $100 per year, and report the name, address, and occupation of any person contributing money or the equivalent in the amount of over $100 per year. Whether the new law succeeds in providing more information than its predecessor depends entirely on whether it is enforced in a radically more serious way than was the earlier legislation. There were no convictions for reporting omissions, which were usual, under the now-repealed Corrupt Practices Act of 1925.[14]

The 1972 law was a rewrite of all federal campaign finance rules. It removed some old unenforced limits on spending and giving—such as the Hatch Act's spending limit of $10,000 for a House of Representatives candidate and $25,000 for a Senate candidate—and substituted new types of limits.* A complementary law provided limited tax credit for persons making po-

---

* Under the law, the only limit on giving is that a candidate cannot spend more than $25,000 of his own money for a House campaign ($35,000 for the Senate and $50,000 for the Presidency or Vice-Presidency), and the only limit on spending concerns what can be spent on communications media. Corporate and union institutional giving remain illegal. For a full summary and analysis of the reforms of 1971–1972, see Chapter Seven: Reforms (Again).

litical contributions. None of the changes legislated in 1971 will reduce campaign spending or the flow of elite money into politics; nor, in political fact, were they intended to do so. The primary political purpose of the new legislation was to reverse the decline in popular confidence in the integrity of the electoral process; the new laws contain the promise, though not the probability, of full and accurate public information about the dynamics of campaign funding.

Despite the fact that imperfect information has been a basic condition confronting anyone interested in election financing, a small number of students of political money have investigated the subject persistently, digging out the often obscure federal and state reports and supplementing these data with interviews and circumstantial evidence to give us a much less imperfect picture than we otherwise would have. Recently much of this work has been done by the staff of the Citizens' Research Foundation, whose director, Herbert Alexander, has authored several factually oriented books on campaign money.[15]

Alexander's estimate for grand total actual campaign costs in 1968 was $300 million—$100 million for the Presidential race, $50 million for the Congressional races, and $150 million for subnational campaigns.[16] His estimates for 1964 were $200 million as a grand total and $60 million as the Presidential campaign total.[17] In his landmark study, *The Costs of Democracy,* Alexander Heard estimated total 1956 costs to have been $155 million, up from $140 million in 1952.[18] The estimated total increase in costs from 1952 to 1968—a period of 16 years—was thus well over 100 percent. By contrast, the consumer price index put out by the U.S. government rose by well under 40 percent in the same period. The real increase was, therefore, substantial.

While they represent a notable increase during the 1960's, the aggregate amounts of political spending that we have mentioned are modest totals compared with other types of aggregates—for example, the gross national product, government budgets, and corporate advertising budgets. Sometimes the amounts spent in an individual campaign seem even trivial. Thus, in the six contests for the House of Representatives from Connecticut in 1968, the general election costs for Democratic and Republican candidates alike averaged just over $53,000 per individual.[19] But in 1968, the average family in the country had an income not much over $9,000 per year.[20] So, unless the candidate for a federal office is *much* better off than the majority of people in the society, he is impelled to seek financial help. The crucial question is not the amount raised but its source and political character.

EVERYTHING IS COST, COST, COST

From the candidate's point of view, everything is cost, cost, cost. No political act is not also a financial act. The greater the number of politicians, reporters, and "prominent citizens" who see a candidate, the larger is the amount that has been spent on phone calls and free drinks. The greater the number of voters who see a candidate, the greater the amount that has gone for travel and broadcast expenses.

Moreover, party organizations do not stand ready to pay much of the bill, even in general election campaigns. Persons seeking party nominations must set up private campaign organizations to conduct a campaign for victory in the primary election.* Incumbent office-holders can usually count on informal support from the party organization in the primary, but if there is a vigorous primary contest even the incumbents need to set up their own private campaign organiza-

* The practice of campaigning for nominations has also come to precede party conventions, the method of choosing Presidential nominees and party nominees in a couple of states.

tions. Such organizations, set up by and for the specific candidate, are needed not only to fight elections but also to raise funds. They often remain after the prenomination campaign, parallel to the party organization or imperfectly integrated into it.

State and national party organizations seldom have more than a small fraction of the necessary campaign money for their nominated candidates. Democratic party national committees, for example, made available well under $1 million to Congressional candidates in 1970, when more than $21 million was spent by the candidates' campaign organizations.[21] The national Republican party had more money available in that year—$2.7 million—but again it was but a fraction of the $23 million spent by Republican Congressional candidates.[22] Even when the national party gives special amounts to selected candidates for national office, these candidates raise supplementary money. Millionaire Republican Senatorial candidate George Bush got $110,000 for his 1970 Texas campaign, about as much as any Congressional candidate has ever gotten from a national party, yet he spent almost four times as much on broadcasting alone.[23]

At the Presidential level the Republican party has developed long-range funding devices (and has developed long-term relationships with hired political consultants) to assist present and future Presidential nominees.[24] Nevertheless, most Presidential campaign money in both parties has to be raised for the specific election, and this involves the use, by the successful nominee and his supporters, of private organizations parallel to the party itself. In the final analysis, the American candidate and his supporters have to raise the money themselves at both primary or preconvention and general election stages. They need to set up private campaign organizations not only to wage the campaign but to fund it as well.

The most impressive private campaign organization

in a long time was that constructed by George McGovern and his supporters for their drive for the Democratic Presidential nomination of 1972. McGovern and his supporters drew up their strategic plans more than two years before the convention was to be held. The Senator from South Dakota thus got an early start, although Senator Edmund Muskie actually began somewhat earlier in his efforts. But Muskie relied on endorsements from established party leaders here and there, and did not build a vigorous private campaign organization. He had one, but it was not as strong as McGovern's.

The McGovern organization had a national staff, regional coordinators, and steering committees in most states. At the local level it was manned by many workers, often volunteers attracted to the antiwar stance of the Senator. They canvassed for delegates—not just by talking to voters in primary states, but also by contacting delegates in nonprimary states. McGovern's standing in the general polls was never very high relative to other candidates, but his organization hired a pollster and used his analyses to shape strategy. Financially, a nucleus of businessmen in Washington conducted fund-raising, and a helpfully steady income came in from mass mailings of letters appealing for funds. In primary states, carefully prepared television commercials were used frequently. The organization was centralized at the top, with media, polling and political consultants, and a finance committee, but decentralized into a series of corps of workers operating in the localities where delegates were to be contacted and voters canvassed. McGovern could not have won the nomination had he not possessed the best private campaign organization.

Each step in setting up an organization and executing a political strategy requires money. In 1960 a mass-produced letter to potential voters in the West

Virginia Democratic Presidential primary went out
over the signature of Franklin D. Roosevelt, Jr. The
message from F.D.R.'s son was intended to invoke the
image of the most popular Democratic President of recent history in endorsing John F. Kennedy. The letter
cost the Kennedy campaign organization $13,000.[25]
Kennedy's opponent, Senator Hubert H. Humphrey,
was short of cash and spent not much more than that on
the entire primary, which Kennedy won.

The 1960 nomination drive of the superbly organized Kennedy machine was another example of a successful private organization at the Presidential level. In
addition, the Kennedy campaign came to symbolize
the role of money in politics. According to records of
the Kennedy forces, over $900,000 was spent before
the nomination (and in addition there were the valuable
services of a Kennedy family plane and the aid of several family members working without salary and paying their own expenses).[26] It was, essentially, a mil-
lion-dollar drive; yet in comparison with other campaigns it was actually not a particularly expensive
one.

For example, textbook accounts imply that General
Dwight D. Eisenhower won the Republican nomination
battle against Senator Robert Taft in 1952 because
convention delegates believed "that the general would
have a stronger appeal." [27] But in fact, the centrally organized nomination machine of the Eisenhower forces
spent practically as much as that of the defeated Taft
forces—that is, at least $2.5 million, with additional
millions' worth of free services and goods contributed
to the Eisenhower campaign.[28]

Unless a person is an incumbent or the incumbent's
choice, and often even then, the organizational imperatives are inescapable. Popular or not, the candidate
must organize, and if he has the money to do it well,
popularity may not matter in the end. This is true even

of Congressional and state candidates, since primary election participation is normally quite low and a good organization can produce a relatively large bloc of voters to win the election for a generally nonpopular figure.

Those who lose nomination campaigns organize, too. Interested in the 1968 Republican Presidential nomination, Governor George Romney of Michigan, former head of the American Motors Corporation, set up a private campaign planning group early in 1967. Soon the organization was running monthly costs of $40,000 (over $25,000 for staff salaries alone, almost $6,000 for travel and entertainment, $2,000 for phone expenses, and so on). [29] Romney's total costs for the prenomination campaign, from which he withdrew before the convention, were $1.5 million. Even the losers' efforts have to be funded. Other candidates for major party nominations spent as follows in 1968: [30]

Eugene McCarthy	about	$11,000,000
Richard Nixon	over	10,000,000
Nelson Rockefeller	over	8,000,000
Robert Kennedy	about	7,000,000
Hubert Humphrey	over	4,000,000
Ronald Reagan	about	750,000
Lyndon Johnson	about	450,000
Others	about	200,000

The costs, quite evidently, add up. Money is spent for staff salaries, offices, supplies, and phones; for literature, bumper stickers, buttons, newsletters, newspaper ads, and billboards; for hospitality suites, walkie-talkies, ushers, and hotel rooms at conventions; for polls and associated political market research; for setting up mail drives, rallies, dinners, and other fund-raising efforts; for candidate and staff travel; for precinct canvassers and poll watchers' expenses; and, of course, for radio and television.

BROADCASTING AND THE NEW POLITICS

Most of the money spent in national elections goes for publicity, for "all those media except personal contact which influence the action of the electorate." [31] The chief media of publicity are radio and, especially, television. In the first heavily television-oriented national campaign, that of 1952, 31 percent of the money spent by the national-level Republican committees went for radio and television, while 34 percent was the Democratic rate. [32]

During the 1960's, spot announcements began to replace longer blocs of time, and time bought from local stations began to replace network time in the broadcasting media mix preferred by Presidential campaign organizations. Spot announcements (while relatively expensive at about $60,000 a minute for prime time in 1968) [33] relieve the politician of the need to go beyond a mere pretense of rational discussion of issues.

Total broadcast costs increased only slightly more rapidly than other national-level campaign costs in the 1960's. In 1968, radio and television expenditures of over $8 million by Republican committees constituted 28 percent of their general election costs (directed mainly at the Presidency), while Democratic broadcast expenditures of almost $4 million were 38 percent of general election costs. [34] The broadcast cost figures we have thus far given are only for actual time purchased; they do not include production costs. Herbert Alexander, noting that production costs of one-fourth to one-third should be added to political broadcast charges, concludes "there is no doubt that the largest single factor in campaign costs is related to broadcasting." [35]

Each national election year, broadcast expenditures are higher than the previous election year's costs. Total political broadcast costs in 1970 were $28 to $30 million for the primary and general election campaigns of Congressional candidates, higher than the

Presidential and Congressional election costs of 1968. [36]

The purpose of broadcasting expenditures is to sell the candidate to the people. This is not a matter of making potential voters aware of what the candidate's distinctive philosophy of government is. No federal candidate in recent political history has had a distinctive philosophy; all have been committed to the basic free enterprise—free world ideology of the American status quo. Within this basic ideological framework there are, of course, real differences as to how liberal or conservative policy should be. But even these marginal differences are usually blurred in the broadcast-oriented national campaign, even though candidates themselves may sometimes feel strongly about their views on issues.

The American candidate simply does not stand for a decisive policy in order to see how many voters will accept or reject his politics. This sort of ideological politics—the politics of voter choice among principled parties (conservative, socialist, liberal) has never been practiced here, a fact curiously celebrated by legions of political scientists, and broadcast-oriented campaigning helps keep it that way. The American campaign does not tamper with the basic social conditioning of the voter but organizes its appeals around his/her superficial prejudices, which are carefully researched.

The political broadcasting experts who actually create and manage the radio and television advertising campaigns approach their tasks with apolitical professionalism, whether they work because of or despite personal political commitments.[37] Issues play a role in planning, but as subordinate variables. Within the limits of the candidate's insistence on sticking to particular positions, issues are muddled and manipulated as components of the image.

The selling of an image is actually not a product of the advent of television, but traces back to the heydays of other media—radio and the newspapers. Over half a century ago a journalist commented:

The choice of the voter is not among men whom he knows but among artificial pictures of men whom he does not know. The making and selling of these pictures is the really expensive part of modern campaigning.[38]

All television does is accentuate the importance of image-making and render it more costly.

But the increasing use of hired political consultants promises to make image-making more cost-effective. There is now an industry, a self-styled profession, with its own organization, the American Association of Political Consultants. A 1972 compendium of politicians and political consultants, appropriately entitled *The Political Market-Place,* listed almost 300 firms.[39] One firm, Matt Reese and Associates, advertises these services:

Advance and candidate scheduling
Bond issue and referenda campaigns
Campaign counseling
Campaign management
Demographic and audience research
Election day activities
Issue research
Media planning, coaching, and buying
Opinion polls / survey research
Political party management and organization
Press relations
Public relations
Speech and script-writing
Staff recruitment and organization
Volunteer recruitment and organization
Voter registration drives
Computer letters and direct mail
Computer software services and data processing
Telephone communications consultants

The campaign companies stand ready to help shape the television campaign and, indeed, all aspects of election politicking. On the Republican side the campaign firms tend to work with a relatively well-funded and organized party on a long-run basis, while on the Democratic side the AFL-CIO's Committee on Political Education has the most sophisticated long-range consulting technology (most of the Democratic consulting follows individual candidates). But all factions of both parties are joined by George Wallace's movement and by nonparty organizations (liberal and conservative) in employing the new firms to an increasing degree.[40]

The modern broadcast-oriented campaign relies on what are essentially market research techniques. Polling is the oldest form of political consulting (with the possible exception of speech-writing). Over 1,000 polls were paid for by candidates' organizations in 1968, at an estimated cost of $6 million.[41] Polls, or survey research, are used not just to find out how a candidate stands relative to others in the race, but also to determine strategy. Polling can map the attitudes of the electorate. Models (computerized mathematical representations of poll findings) can be used to test the probable effect of possible appeals to voters. Beginning in 1960, when the Simulmatics Corporation developed a model of the voting public for John Kennedy, increasingly sophisticated audience profiles have been drawn up. The profiles can sort people according to region, religion, income, education, race, sex, etc., and correlate these attributes with the kinds of messages that polls suggest people might like to hear. The appropriate messages can then be provided by the ad campaign, and more polling can be used to follow up and gauge the effectiveness of the ads.

Although it may seem obvious, it needs to be pointed out that the politicians' and their consultants' basic reliance on polling does *not* mean that the people's needs and wishes determine the actual positions and policies of the politicians. In the first place and most obviously, vague promises scientifically proffered to this or that social group can, as everyone understands, be ignored or explained away when the candidate is in office.

But something even more basic is involved: what polls never do is suggest alternatives that "responsible" politicians and publicists have not been discussing. Polls probe feelings within a vocabulary of alternatives that safely skirts the basic structure of power in the society. Part of the conservative safety of the polls is due to the difficulty that many respondents have in understanding the systemic sources of their everyday frustrations, but another, and the greater, part is due to the framing of the questions themselves, in which the obviously decent and democratic answer appears as the most extreme position in a range of choices, if indeed it appears at all. Polling is not designed to alter the basic commitment of all persons who manage to get as far as candidacy for a major office to the existing politicoeconomic order. A fundamental alternative is excluded from polls, as it is from political campaigns generally.*

The polling, the broadcast spending, the canvassing—all are oriented toward winning partial control of the minds of people without proposing changes in the existing class power structure. It is not surprising that the greatest twentieth-century leaps in national political expenditures have occurred in Presidential election years characterized by quite widespread popular unrest—1936 and 1968 (see Chart I). It is precisely in such times that various factions in the established parties struggle most vigorously to win the people over to their versions of the basic ideology, and that the interest of various factions of the elite in campaign funding is at its peak.

* See Chapter Six: The Excluded Alternative.

RAISING POLITICAL MONEY

A central function of the political "parties" and, more importantly, of the paraparty private campaign organizations of U.S. politics is collecting funds for use in running the modern media-oriented campaign. For the modern politicians one of the most desirable methods of fund-raising is the direct mail appeal. Lists of potential givers are built up. These lists can be developed from party lists of prospective givers, or bought from organizations with donor and subscription lists, such as charities and magazines. Letters can then be sent en masse to the names on the list, incorporating appeals for funds. For the personal touch, computerized machines can type the addressee's name into the very body of the letter, and first-class (rather than bulk rate) postage can be used.

Direct mail came of age in the Republican campaign of 1964. As many big givers switched to the Democratic presidential nominee in aversion to GOP nominee Barry Goldwater, apparently seen as a dangerously independent maverick by some, an unprecedented amount of money came in by mail—almost $6 million for all national Republican committees. To get this return, 15 million pieces of fund-raising literature had to be sent out.[42]

The Goldwater lists had been adapted from those the Republican National Committee had earlier begun to develop, and they later formed a nucleus around which continuing mail drives by Republican committees could be built. Richard Nixon used mailings in his nomination drive in 1968, and for the whole election Republican committees sent out 22 million mailings and got $6.6 million back. Even more Republican money was raised this way in 1972.[43]

Like Goldwater in 1964, Democrat George McGovern was seen by some in 1972 as a dangerously independent sort, but of a liberal rather than a conservative type. Indeed, both Goldwater and McGovern were called "radical" during their nomination drives. In reality, they both were deeply committed to the state-supported capitalist economy. But the big givers are in a position to use their money to punish candidates even whose mere rhetoric drifts too far from the political center. A relative (but far from absolute) scarcity of big backers forced McGovern to rely somewhat more heavily than usual on mail solicitation, and he stated that more than 150,000 people gave to his prenomination campaign.[44] McGovern was perfectly willing to accept huge gifts from the corporate rich, but he turned necessity into virtue by claiming, on the basis of the mail drives, that his candidacy was being democratically financed.

In actuality the mail drives have never been sufficient to fund any candidate's campaign. They have always been supplements to a variety of other fund-raising methods. Politicians often address fund-raising dinners at $100 a plate (or less—or much, much more). In the telethon, gifts are usually called in to a televised operations center. The mass rallies held by George Wallace and Eugene McCarthy in 1968 were innovations in fund-raising, as were the benefit concerts given by rock music stars for McGovern in 1972. Finally, there is direct personal solicitation by workers in the candidate's campaign organization or by the candidate himself.

Personal solicitation is essential for really big gifts. And the big givers, in turn, are needed to get a campaign organized. Their money is needed to finance small-collection fund-raising efforts. Direct mail, for example, cost $1 million for the Republicans in 1964, and over $1.5 million in 1968.[45] A mailing of 5 million pieces just after McGovern's 1972 nomination cost his organization $700,000, and it was the $2 million that was given, loaned, or pledged to McGovern by big givers during the week of the convention that enabled him to send out the massive mailing.[46] Marvin Rosenberg, the New York manufacturer who served as Hubert Humphrey's main fund-raiser in 1968, has said that "you have to have the [early] money before the campaign is underway to make any impact, to do any travelling, hire any staff, buy any television time." [47] And, we might add, to raise more money.

At the middle-class grass roots level it is volunteers or party workers who actually collect the relatively small gifts. But this personal solicitation, like all fund-raising efforts, is generally managed by businessmen; for both Democrats and Republicans, most solicitors have been, as Heard put it, "successful businessmen." [48] Since each party protects the interests of corporate property there is no reason to be surprised that businessmen raise money for each.

The managers of solicitation do not leave the big fish to the volunteers; they go direct. The corporate rich tap others in their business and social circles on an informal basis in the course of normal interaction, and they supplement these contacts with exclusive cocktail parties especially designed to raise political money. The candidate's agent will set the example by pledging thousands (or tens of thousands or hundreds of thousands) of dollars of his money, and later will personally follow up on the pledges others have made. To tap the bigger givers, our businessman/solicitor will have to bring along his candidate, or at the very least have him call. Indeed, national candidates spend a great deal of personal time selling themselves to corporate political bankrollers. Such candidates are not a threat to the corporate system.

SOURCES OF MONEY
There is no such thing as a definitive map of the socio-economic origins of political money. We do know that

the rate of political contribution, like the rate of participation in the established governmental system generally, rises with income. The results of a Survey Research Center poll analyzed by Heard were as
follows: [49]

Annual Family Income	Percent Giving, 1952	Percent Giving, 1956
Less than $3,000	2	2
$3,000–4,999	3	6
$5,000–7,499	7	12
$7,500–9,999	14	17
$10,000 and over	17	31

In other words, of people in a national sample who
said their family income was less than $3,000, 2 percent
also said they gave something to politics, and so on. We
took the last Presidential election year SCR survey
available, that of 1968, and obtained analagous data,
as follows: [50]

Annual Family Income	Percent Giving, 1968
Less than $4,000	3
$4,000–5,999	4
$6,000–8,999	7
$9,000–11,999	8
$12,000–24,999	12
$25,000 and over	31

Of those in the top SRC income class who said they
voted for Wallace in 1968, 20 percent said they gave
money to politics, while the rates of contribution for
Nixon and Humphrey voters in that category were 39
and 40 percent, respectively. But relatively rich people
gave at a much higher rate than poor people, irrespective of candidate preference.

SRC income breakdowns do not go very high in the

income structure due to the relatively small population that are very rich, but the survey results do suggest that the higher the income the higher the likelihood of political contribution. This conforms to common sense.

In 1959 the *Harvard Business Review* mailed a questionnaire to a cross-section of subscribers and got 2,700 responses (of 10,000 polled) from what were held to be "top executives." Fifty-four percent of the respondents said that they had personally given money to a political campaign in 1958 (a non-Presidential year) and over a quarter said they had personally worked in a campaign.[51] Going further up the economic scale, 70 percent of the few very richest people are on record as having contributed to politics in 1968, and probably even more of them did so.[52]

Much of our information about sources of money comes from the reports that have been filed in imperfect conformity with imperfect laws, and evasions of these laws are pretty common. Some evasion has been legal. The biggest political dinner yet held in America grossed $2.6 million for the Republicans in 1969, but it was held in Washington, D.C., where there was no reporting law, and the only list of ticket buyers went directly to Richard M. Nixon. Republican committees set up in Illinois in 1969 and Washington in 1970 (like the District of Columbia, Illinois had no reporting law) raised, divided up, and transferred money from unknown givers to other geographical districts, nicely circumventing existing state and federal laws.[53]

Before the reporting provisions of the Federal Election Campaign Act of 1971 became effective in April 1972, Republican fund-raisers built up a cache of many millions. The Fluor Corporation's vice-chairman, a party fund-raiser, warned potential donors of the imminence of disclosure "which," as he told his peers, "we all naturally want to avoid." [54]

In the 1968 general election campaign, the Democratic national committees received more money from sources not subject to federal disclosure law than from covered sources. And despite the voluntary listing of the names of a small group of the corporate rich who loaned over $3 million to the Humphrey campaign, almost half of the more than $14 million received came from persons whose names are not known. Millions were received in a mysterious category called "constructive receipts" and through intricate transfers from committees based in states where they were not subject to reporting laws.[55]

Some evasion is illegal, but little has been done about it. When the Clerk of the House of Representatives referred to the Justice Department the names of over 100 House candidates who had either failed to file required reports or who had missed deadlines for filing in 1968, the Department observed that there was no precedent for prosecution and dropped the cases.[56] The same good fortune awaited some 30 nonfilers of 1970.

We have already observed that political money raised in cash leaves no records if the politician fails to identify the source. Other means of escaping public identification of fund sources have included giving many small gifts just below the federal reporting threshold, making unreported (and later forgiven) loans, and, for corporations, providing free services to candidates.

With these serious limitations in mind, what do official records tell us about the sources of political money? Official national level records filed with Congress for Humphrey, Nixon, and Wallace committees for 1968 indicate that 51 percent of all money raised by these units from individuals' contributions came from people giving $100 or more.[57] The proportion of income from individual gifts of $500 and over, a very tiny fraction of all individuals' gifts, was 42 percent.[58]

These figures do not mean that even 49 percent of national political money came from "small" contributors of $99 or less because the official figures are quite incomplete. Politicians always emphasize the number of small contributors to their campaigns, but they are never anxious to fully disclose the role of the big rich in finance in the reports they file. In 1968 the prenomination campaigns were not covered by reporting law, but it is known that the role of big givers was even more important than in the postconvention period.[59]

Rich businessmen are not the only big givers. Union leaders, prohibited from contributing out of dues money, have developed a simple device. "Voluntary" contributions from members go into a political fund controlled by the leaders. Technically, labor political spending is an expression of many small givers, and labor spending certainly is not listed as individual giving by this or that official. But political reality is something else, and will require a separate summary of the unions' role in our later discussion of liberalism.* The millions that various union committees spend, suffice it to note here, are but a fraction of the corporate input.

While the importance of the corporate rich to political finance does not spring from their providing any specific fraction of money, but rather from their being courted by all factions of the established parties and, most crucially, by liberal nonincumbents getting their campaigns started, it does appear that most national money clearly comes from the big contributors.

This raises an interesting problem. Are the many thousands of people who are known to have given $100 or more to national politics definitely members of the business class, let alone of the corporate rich? It is theoretically possible that givers of $100—or even the 13,000 nationally recorded givers of $500 or more in 1968—come from a broad spectrum of the middle

* See Chapter Five: Financing Liberalism.

class and simply represent people especially concerned about politics. What *is* the relationship between
the political finance elite and the corporate economic
elite?

It appears to be one of very substantial overlap. We
know that the rate of contribution rises with income. We
know that 484 known givers of $10,000 and up in 1968
gave at the very least more than $12 million to Demo-
cratic and Republican committees.[60] These were all
members of the corporate rich. Finally, we conducted
an analysis of the big 1968 givers from Cleveland, Ohio,
and our results suggest substantial overlap.

Working from the names on file with Congress as
givers of $100 or more, researchers have been publish-
ing lists of those who gave $500 or more. We decided to
work with the last published Presidential year list of big
givers available, the Citizens' Research Foundation's
list of 1968 givers.[61] As small a fraction of all givers (let
alone all voters) as this list contains, it still has several
thousand names, so we decided to select from the list
and work only with the names of givers from the Cleveland metropolitan area. We analyzed the backgrounds
of all those known (from the CFR list) to have given
$500 or more to national politics from the four counties
comprising the metropolitan area.[62]

Research resulted in positive identification of all but
nine of 187 big Cleveland givers of 1968. (Combinations of children living with a parent, and/or of hus-
bands and wives, were counted as single contributors
for purposes of analysis.) Of the 178 identified house-
holds from which a known contribution came, the head in
virtually every case was or had been a businessman.
The only exceptions were a successful author, a retired
military officer, and a person reported as a factory worker
(but whose address was an office in a downtown business building).[63]

Moreover, the Cleveland contributors were, as a

group, corporate directors. They were also corporate officers; very few were only directors or only officers. Considering major current occupations (or the last major current occupation of the household head in the case of retired persons or widows making contributions), over three-quarters of these national-level givers were corporate officers or directors. Most of the rest were partners in stock brokerage firms or law firms. (The occupations of a few heirs or heiresses could not be located in published sources. Only a very few of the Cleveland group were doctors or proprietors.) [64]

Most of the lawyers in the Cleveland study were found to be among the givers who occupied corporate controlling positions—that is, they were also directors or officers or both. Long ago C. Wright Mills wrote that "the lawyer is becoming a pivotal figure in the giant corporation" [65] and that:

The inner core of the power elite also includes men of the higher legal and financial type from the great law factories and investment firms, who are almost professional go-betweens of economic, political and military affairs. . . .[66]

The corporate rich include not only industrialists and financiers but also lawyers like John W. Reavis, managing partner of the Cleveland law firm Jones, Day, Cockley & Reavis. In 1968 Reavis was a director of several of the country's biggest corporations, including Westinghouse, the seventeenth largest industrial firm and a big war contractor, and his law partners were on the boards of several other top corporations.[67] By 1971 his law firm's members sat on the boards of a total of 25 corporations (and, incidentally, received more than $2 million in legal fees from interlocking corporations).[68] Reavis was a member of Cleveland's exclusive Union Club. By social and corporate position Reavis was a member of the ruling class. He appeared on our list of

Cleveland givers along with five of his law partners; collectively they gave $7,500 to Republican committees.

Indeed, most of the Cleveland contributors were members of the ruling class. Most were members of the social upper class based on the corporate rich, and a larger number were members of the social elite and/or officers or directors of the top banks and corporations of America.[69] (This majority emerged even though the social and business backgrounds of some of the givers from wealthy and prominent local families could not be located in the published indicators we used.)

Whatever the boundary line at which contributions tend to come more from the middle classes than from the corporate rich, it is apparently below $500.[70] The Cleveland study suggests that the contributions of $500 or more to national-level committees in 1968 exclusively represented the business class financing elections, with most of the funds actually coming from the corporate rich.[71] The backgrounds of those who give big money at the national level are probably not only business class, but also more often than not ruling class backgrounds.

In a recent poll only 8 percent of the people stated that anyone in their families had contributed any money in any way to politics at any level in 1968.[72] The vast majority of people, understandably, have nothing to do with financing the existing parties. The rate of contribution rises with income, and most of the money in national politics comes from the big contributors. The big contributors are the business class, and most of the money they place into politics is given by the corporate rich.

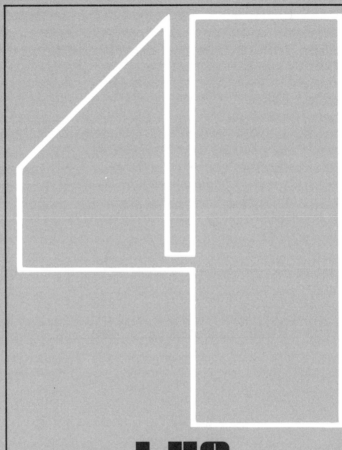

the
corporate
input

In 1907 corporate political contributions to federal elections were outlawed. For the more sincere of the reformers, the prohibition was part of a general attempt to dismantle the politicoeconomic power of the rising financial and industrial capitalists and to restore a measure of balance among socioeconomic classes in American society. But as the strategy of anticorporate progressivism failed in general, so the particular provision regarding corporate contributions—which is still part of the law—has been so systematically circumvented as to be but a propagandistic formality.

Many are the legal and illegal forms of giving at the disposal of those who control the corporate world. Every four years they support the two established parties by investing in tax-deductible advertising in national convention program books. Proceeds from this advertising have amounted to up to $1.5 million for the Democrats (in 1964) [1] and $1.7 million for the Republicans (in 1972).[2] Party convention financing also benefits from tax-deductible gifts from local business leaders in the host city; in Chicago in 1968 about $400,000 was raised for the Democratic convention, principally at one meeting in the Mayor's office.[3]

The role of corporate money in funding conventions came to public attention in 1972 when it was discovered that International Telephone and Telegraph Corporation had pledged up to $400,000 toward the Republican convention's costs in San Diego, following which the Justice Department dropped an antimerger suit against ITT.[4] The convention was then moved to Miami to escape the associations of the now-withdrawn offer, but it was financed in the same way—just not by ITT. The ITT incident should not obscure the fact that corporate backing for the parties as such is not designed just to get particular favors from politicians. The funding is often "bipartisan"—Miami interests chipped in for two party conventions in 1972, and many corporations buy space in both parties' program books —and in any case is conditional on the fact that neither party ever challenges the big corporate system as such. The advertising and the contributions reward this reliability, and all members of the corporate rich benefit from them.

The two-party system works so well that the advertising industry has given many millions of dollars' worth of free advertising in national bipartisan drives urging people to register, vote, and give money—"to the party of your choice." The choice, in reality, is very slight indeed, in view of the absolutely basic partisan agreement on corporate prerogatives shared by both parties. "Bipartisan" efforts are really monopartisan.

In another form of giving, corporate leaders regularly dun middle-management employees for contributions to campaign funds to be distributed by top management. This form of corporate spending appears on public reports, if at all, as the gifts of specific individuals, not the corporate heads. These internal funds are analagous to those that union leaders collect, except that they come from supervisory and managerial personnel rather than from rank and file workers. The existence of the funds is routinely denied by corporate spokesmen. Morton Mintz and Jerry Cohen, however, have described a letter sent by two vice-presidents of Sterling Drug to more than 500 of its executives, asking for contributions of $30 to $200. The letter, dated August 7, 1970, read in part:

> [W]e have many *friends of* both *parties—important to industry in general and* very *important to the advancement of our industry and through it to the advancement of the public welfare.* . . . *Sterling* . . . may not, *under the law, contribute to political campaigns. So* . . . *we must do what most other corporations do—go to the key members of the corporate* team *for help.* . . .
> *Specifically, we're asking for a* voluntary *contribution*

*from you for a political fund to be allocated to those legisla-
tors at the Federal and State level, be they Democrats or Republicans, whose re-election or election is important to our
industry and to* Sterling Drug, Inc.[5]

Other such letters have become public, but it is not
possible to state definitively how prevalent the practice is. It appears to be very widespread, especially
among big firms. A recent study reported by Walter
Pincus has detailed several such funds and variants
thereof.[6] Some corporations provide salary incre-
ments, bonuses, or attorney's fees with the understanding that they will then be placed as "individual"
contributions to specified candidates.[7]

Reported gifts to national committees by top officers and directors are often big enough to get publicity. *Congressional Quarterly* reported that 11 officers
and directors of Litton Industries gave over $150,000 to
the Republicans in 1968, when Litton was the four-
teenth largest of the war/atomic energy/space contractors. Nineteen Ford Motor Company officials gave
$53,000 to Democratic committees and over $87,000 to
Republican committees. Six Avco Corporation princi-
pals gave $13,000 to Democratic committees and
$3,000 to Republican committees, 12 IBM officials
gave over $136,000 across party lines, etc.[8]

If enforced, the Federal Election Campaign Act of
1971 will cast additional light on corporate funding of
Congressional candidates. It is likely, however, that
tracing corporate gifts in Congressional campaigns
will continue to require detailed research. For example, Dennis M. Callahan went to the Ohio state capitol
to examine records which showed that Representative
J. William Stanton, who in 1970 had voted to kill a Congressional investigation of the banking lobby, received
contributions from 14 officers of the First National City
Bank of New York for the 1970 campaign, from seven
officers of a bank holding company, and from several

other bankers. The sums were relatively small, ranging from $10 to $500, but they added up to a banking input of over $3,000 for the general election.[9] In addition, the Bankers' Political Action Committee (BANKPAC) reported a $2,500 gift to Stanton.[10] Special interest funding is a basic fact of Congressional political life, and the gifts received often amount to much more than they did in the Stanton case.

Businessmen routinely fund Congressmen who protect their interests in the legislative process. For this purpose they are increasingly turning to political action committees like BANKPAC. Another big committee, broader in scope, is Business-Industry Political Action Committee. These committees often encourage contributions in checks of $100 so as to just avoid federal reporting requirements.

Corporations regularly provide valuable services to politicians. In 1972, candidate George Wallace got a lowered rental rate on his leased plane.[11] Others have gotten free travel, free hotel suites, free billboard space, and the free services of corporate employees —all paid for by the corporation in obvious, if unprosecuted, violation of federal law.[12] Corporations have paid legislators inflated honoraria (another type of disguised gift). They have often extended credit to candidates, with no realistic basis for expecting repayment; extensive debts of Democratic Presidential committees and politicians in the late 1960's were settled at from 25 to 36 cents per dollar.

The various forms of corporate giving, ranging from the covert raising of slush funds to advance industry interests to "bipartisan" (really monopartisan) encouragement of employee participation in electoral politics (a frequent corporate mission),[13] all support and help to protect the corporate system as such. The simplest, or at any rate most direct, way in which those who have a controlling economic position in society can go about protecting the existing power structure ("the free enterprise system") through the use of their money is to pay directly—to make an individual personal political contribution. Such personal contributions may produce the greatest part of the pool of corporate money in electoral politics, and at any rate they are the most thoroughly documented corporate input.

The corporate rich and their forerunners have long given personally to politics. In 1896, when the Democrats ran William Jennings Bryan on his populist platform, Republican tycoon–fund-raiser Mark Hanna drummed up financing for *his* candidate, William McKinley, not only by systematically assessing industrialists and bankers with a particular vested interest in government policy outcomes, but also by appealing to propertied interests to protect the very security and structure of the business system.* If it is doubtful that Bryan really did threaten the business system as such, nevertheless Hanna raised enormous sums for McKinley, while Bryan was relatively strapped for funds.[14]

In 1904, most of the Democratic Presidential fund was supplied by two rich men (August F. Belmont and Thomas F. Ryan).[15] In 1936, two of the most important big propertied American families, the du Ponts and the Pews, together gave over $1 million to the Republican fund.[16] But the burden of financing has usually been spread fairly widely among the rich. There is hardly a well-known person in the history of twentieth-century business who is not known to have contributed big

---

* Hanna's appeal again demonstrates the dual and perhaps inextricable motives for ruling class political financing. One motive is not directly related to class-wide interests but has to do with protecting the interests of the particular corporations in the political process. On this particularistic purpose nearly all reformers have focused their critical attention. This makes it all the more important to underline the other purpose, which is implicit in seeking protection for one firm in the system but is also sometimes explicit as well—to protect the big property system as such.

sums to national politics—Armour, Astor, Benton, Dreyfus, Lehman, Field, Ford, McCormick, Frick, Kaiser, and so on—and alongside the well-known names are many more that are less well known.

FINANCING REPUBLICANS

The role of the corporate rich in funding Democrats, particularly of the liberal variety, is more significant in the continuation of the existing oligarchy than is their role in funding Republicans, but a few observations about the Grand Old Party are in order.

It has been estimated that, outside the South, 80 to 90 percent of the U.S. upper class are Republicans.[17] Financing patterns show a Republican preference among the corporate rich. The few very richest men in America made substantial Democratic contributions in 1968, but spent many times more money funding Republican national committees.[18] In our study of Cleveland big givers, only 15 percent were found to have contributed to national Democratic committees in 1968.[19] Republican funding benefits from the participation of a broad spectrum of the corporate rich. Despite their efficient and very productive mail-solicitation machine, the reports of national-level Republican committees show that even more money is raised from the big givers.* GOP Congressional and Presidential committees are virtually never short of cash (Democratic ones often seem to be).

Contenders for the Republican Presidential nomination always get funding from the corporate rich. The image of the Republican party as a party of big business is as apt as the image of the Democrats as a party opposed to big business is inappropriate. Examples of

* A probable exception is 1964, when most funds may have come from givers of less than $100.

big Republican funders are bound to be somewhat arbitrary, but a couple may be useful.[20]

David Rockefeller is best known as the chairman of the board of directors of one of the world's biggest financial institutions, New York's Chase Manhattan Bank. The bank's directors sit on many other big corporate boards; the bank's $14 billion in trust assets encompasses many big corporate stocks; and the bank has many billions of dollars' worth of loans outstanding to business. Rockefeller owns millions of dollars' worth of the Chase Manhattan Corporation's stock (the corporation is the Bank's holding company) and is its largest individual stockholder; his family as a group owns 5 percent (a controlling interest) of the stock. Chase Manhattan's influence is international in scope, with more than 40 foreign branch banks and thousands of correspondent banks around the world. Rockefeller is also a director of the Chase International Development Corporation, the Banque de Commerce (Antwerp), and Chase Manhattan Bank, Geneva; and he is a partner in assorted real estate ventures. But he is not only a banker-businessman.

David Rockefeller is also a philanthropist. He was, as of 1971, the chairman of the Donations Committee of Near East Emergency Donations; president of the Rockefeller Family Fund; vice-chairman of the Rockefeller Brothers Fund (with assets of some $200 million in 1969); and president of the Seatlantic Fund.

Rockefeller is also an educator—trustee of the University of Chicago (begun in the late nineteenth century with John D. Rockefeller's plentiful seed money) and chairman of Rockefeller University. Then, too, as chairman of the Museum of Modern Art in New York City and as a director of the Business Committee for the Arts, he is involved in cultural affairs.

Rockefeller's involvement in civic affairs is, most importantly, as chairman of the Council on Foreign Relations, Inc., which, as Domhoff has shown, represents an important agency through which the views of the corporate rich and their representatives are translated into governmental foreign policy.[21] Rockefeller's foreign policy views, which are embodied in U.S. policy, show a special concern for Latin America, where much of the Rockefeller family fortune is rooted:

The private capital which Latin America so badly needs will be attracted to the area only if it is given credible assurance that equitable repatriation of profits will be possible.[22]

The above do not exhaust Rockefeller's interests and affiliations. (The corporate rich are not only economically powerful; they also dominate the boards of directors of major charitable, educational, and policy-formulating institutions in America. Through the foundations which fund research and through such key policy associations as the CFR, the corporate rich are in a superb position to participate in the shaping both of the general ideological climate and of particular government policy lines. There is nothing conspiratorial about the broad-based institutional power of the corporate rich, although there does seem to be a conspiracy of silence among respectable commentators in the face of such obviously significant power.) In addition to the roles we have been discussing, Rockefeller participates directly in governmental affairs. He has been consulted by U.S. Presidents and has served on scores of advisory committees. And, finally, he gives regularly to politics. No one knows the grand total of his gifts, but he is on record as having given well over $10,000 to the Republicans every Presidential year from 1952 through 1972. In 1968 he also gave the Humphrey campaign $5,000. The amounts, for Rockefeller, are as nothing, and they certainly do not compare with the $1.5 million that public records show his mother spent to help finance his brother Nelson's campaign for the 1968

Presidential nomination.[23] But for the Republican politicians, the big gifts are welcome and they add up fast.

David Rockefeller is one of the more prominent and influential of the elite. But not all corporate rich GOP bankrollers are so well known. One of the many who, according to filed reports, gave more than did Rockefeller in 1968 is Vernon Stouffer, chairman of the Food Services Group of the Litton Industries conglomerate. He owns millions of dollars worth of Litton stock (and in addition was paid a salary of $36,000 plus pension benefits in 1969,[24] a relatively low big-corporation salary). Stouffer is also a stockholder and director in Republic Steel, and sits on the boards of two more of the top corporations—United Air Lines and Consolidated Natural Gas Company of New York. He dabbles in charity as a trustee of University Hospitals of Cleveland and as president of the Vernon Stouffer Foundation and the Stouffer Foods Corporation Fund. In addition, he owned the Cleveland Indians baseball club. Little known, like most members of the corporate rich, Stouffer has the characteristic multiple interests—stockholding *and* corporate control positions in *several* corporations *plus* outside institutional interests. We have listed only his principal affiliations—and he is only one among thousands of big backers of Republican candidates.

It would be wrong, in noting that the great majority of the ruling class consider themselves Republican, to create the impression of inflexible loyalty to that party as such. No doubt there are a great many dyed-in-the wool Republican tycoons who give to the party as such and would not do otherwise. But we don't know exactly how many fit that mold, and as time goes on an increasing number, even if still a minority, of the corporate rich and the business class in general have been won away from the strict conservatism of their fathers and have adopted a more moderate and flexible stance toward state programs purportedly designed to regulate industry and alleviate social insecurity. It was the more liberal and far-seeing members of the elite who from the very beginning of this century had led the way toward ideological flexibility. The peak of contributions to the Democrats came in 1964, but every year many of the big rich support both parties. David Rockefeller was not alone in splitting his contribution in 1968; over 250 contributors are known to have given $500 or more to national committees of both parties in 1968,[25] and many more probably did so through unreported channels. Henry Ford II, chairman of the board of the Ford Motor Company, gave $30,000 Democratic and $7,250 Republican dollars in 1968; wealthy Republican investment banker C. Douglas Dillon, who sits on the Chase Manhattan Bank board with David Rockefeller and is also a stockholder and director of American Telephone and Telegraph Company, contributed to Humphrey's nomination drive in 1972, then gave to the Nixon organization in the general election campaign.[26] Dillon, who held office in the Eisenhower Administration and was Secretary of the Treasury in the Kennedy and Johnson Administrations, gave $42,000 to the Democrats in 1964 but contributed thousands to Republicans before and after that.

Thus, the general conservatism of the corporate rich gives way to split contributions, to straight Democratic contributions, as we shall see, and even to liberal contributions. But elite financing did not go in any great amounts to the reactionary Wallace movement of 1964–1972. Wallace was, of course, a Democrat when not an Independent, but his ideological approach, like that of many Southern Democrats, more closely resembled Republican conservatism than it did liberalism. Most of Wallace's big money in 1968 came from Alabama, Texas, and Florida, but most of his money was not big.[27] In fact, according to the records of the Wallace campaign, three-quarters of the money for 1968

was raised from individual contributions of less than
$100. Not that Wallace did not seek big gifts and get
some; his organization set up a Patriot's Club for givers
of $1,000 and more, he was able to give $1,000-a-plate
dinners, and he received some 500 contributions of
$500 and up, thus raising about a half-million dollars
from among the conservative (and largely Southern)
rich. But in 1968, as today, the corporate rich were un-
ready to encourage an independent right-wing movement outside the framework of the two major parties in
whose financing and in whose Administrations they
have been so heavily involved.

FINANCING DEMOCRATS

Republicans and Democrats are agreed on the present
form of government in this society and on the structure
of privileges embodied in the big property system. We
make distinctions among reactionaries, conservatives,
and liberals in the two parties, but in reality all three
types agree on basic principles in the sense that they
are committed to the existing order—governmental as
well as corporate. All three are really varieties of conservative. There are differences, sometimes intense,
as to what should be the specific content and manner of
administration of social policy and civil and criminal
law. It is this range of safely limited opinion to which
students have traditionally been introduced in civics
classes and college courses, though they increasingly
threaten to go beyond their indoctrination. The most
general characterization of the differences among the
conservatives is that reactionaries would like to see
change in the direction of greater repression of political dissent and social discontent, while liberals would
like to see change in the direction of greater toleration
of dissent and greater concessions to discontent.

The Democratic party contains reactionary, "conservative," and liberal types of conservatives. If the traditional conservatism of the party as a whole sometimes became enlightened enough, in this or that office, to enact those minimal concessions to popular aspirations that earn the party recognition as the more liberal of the two, these concessions were always based on explicit rejection of any assault on the illegitimate economic power system which is the actual structural source of popular insecurity and alienation. Politicians in the Democratic party have pursued a conservative social policy at all levels and times; big property remains sacred.

When the Presidential candidates of the Democratic party have adopted slightly antibig property rhetoric, as in 1896 and 1936, they have suffered desertions—but never total abandonment—by backers. For many, many years the corporate rich have contributed substantially to Democratic financing, even though the elite as a group have almost always given more to Republican campaigns.

Interestingly, it is not a broad cross-section of the corporate rich that finances the Democrats. It is true that a small number of Protestant patricians have backed Democratic candidates financially—givers from such families as the Biddles, Fords, Harrimans, du Ponts, and even Rockefellers—but the bulk of the funds from big donors comes from a couple of locales and a cluster of interests within the corporate world.

In a recent analysis based on a study of the backgrounds of the biggest long-term national-level reported Democratic givers, Domhoff generalized about the Democratic party's big backers. Domhoff first argued that, on the basis of patterns of interlocking corporate directorships and other business and friendship bonds, there is a clique or interest group within the corporate economy whose major controlling personnel are "the Jewish businessmen of New York and the

Cowboy oilmen of Texas." [28] He then concluded that, while this interest group includes only a few very large corporations (such as Ford), it is the source of the single most important bloc of Democratic cash. In addition, the key Democratic fund-raisers are Jewish businessmen in such cities as New York, Chicago, Los Angeles, and San Francisco.

Domhoff did not argue that the great bulk of Jewish businessmen are Democratic, only that the great bulk of all other top businessmen are Republican, so that the money raised by the Jewish funders and some of their business associates is quite critical for Democratic candidates. In short, the most important Democratic funders and fund-raisers are "Jewish investment bankers from Wall Street, along with their business clients in major states such as California, Texas, and Illinois. . . ." [29]

Herbert Alexander, too, has pointed to the key importance of Wall Street money for the Democrats, whose fat cats he sees as coming from a narrow base in the corporate world, particularly from among the nouveaux riches.[30] Alexander assesses southern California money as an especially important supplement to the critical New York money.

The Democratic party is not a very cohesive entity, and its greatest unity may lie in the dependence of its important candidates on big financial backers of the sort identified here. But to talk of "Jewish" and "Wall Street" money is not to suggest that some secret conspiracy with distinctive interests controls the party. There are, after all, plenty of givers like Corliss Lamont, the leftish philosopher of patrician origins who gave thousands to George McGovern in 1972; he obviously does not represent Jewish or nouveau-riche money.[31] In fact, to identify the biggest single loose group of Democratic backers is simply to illuminate the realities of election financing. New or old, Republican or Democrat, Jewish or gentile, Wall Street or Detroit, members of the corporate rich share an interest in the big property structure which makes them a ruling class. Indeed, that is precisely the point: Democratic candidates are financially quite dependent on members of the corporate rich for campaign funds.

Thus, in order to be the front-runner for the Presidential nomination in 1972, Senator Edmund Muskie had to send one of the corporate businessmen raising money for him to eight New York millionaires in late 1969; their pledges of $200,000 made it possible to begin the drive for the nomination.[32] Eventually more than four hundred people gave Muskie $1,000 or more in his unsuccessful drive.[33]

One of the big Muskie backers was Lionel I. Pincus. Pincus, president of the New York investment banking firm E. M. Warburg, Pincus & Company owns millions of dollars' worth of stock and sits on the boards of at least seven corporations. He is also the president of the Lionel I. Pincus Foundation. One of the companies on whose board Pincus sits is, curiously, called the City Investing Company. In actuality City Investing is a top manufacturing corporation producing, among other things, napalm and anti-personnel weapons for the war against Indochina.[34]

Of course, the Democrats were out of the White House when Muskie and all the other serious contenders and their financial angels began to line up for the 1972 convention. But when the political resources of an incumbent President were at the disposal of the party in 1961–1968, national-level fund-raising relied even more heavily on the big givers. Democratic finances in the Kennedy and Johnson administrations reflected the shallow depth of actual popular commitment to the party, and they help to further underline the party's de facto role as an agency of the ruling class. The President's Club was a key set of political committees during this period. (It was Franklin D. Roosevelt who had the first Presidential financial organ, the One Thousand Club.) [35] In the Kennedy and Johnson administrations the President's Clubs of givers of $1,000 or more were revived. Drives to enroll many regularly contributing Democrats were given up. Saloma and Sontag write:

> The President's Club, the effective finance arm of the Democratic party, turned the focus of Democratic finances to sizable gifts from a smaller group of individuals. The club raised enormous amounts for the party in the mid-1960's. In 1966, for example, the President's Club for Johnson Committee reported receipts of $2,732,577, the largest single addition to the party's coffers that year.[36]

The chairman of the national President's Club in the mid-1960's was Arthur Krim, perpetual big political giver and chairman of the board of United Artists.* By 1968, Democratic nominee Humphrey's campaign was being financed in the same way as his preconvention campaign—that is, almost entirely by big contributors, including 43 persons who made loans totaling over $3 million.[37] Calling it "ironic that a party with as large an electoral base as the Democratic has not been able to tap its constituents for large sums in small packages," Alexander concluded:

> Instead of using their eight years of White House power and prestige to build a solid financial structure with hundreds of thousands of party supporters, the Democrats had turned to a handful of rich contributors, White House social patronage, and corporate advertising.[38]

The reality of the critical financial input of the corporate rich to the Democratic party is undeniable. If anything, their money is more vital to Democrats than to Republicans. In view of this fact there is really nothing

* United Artists itself took full-page ads at $10,000 and $15,000 per page in the 1964 and 1968 convention program books.

ironic about the failure of the working man to fund "his" party, which does not stand for his liberation. If anything is ironic, it is the willingness of so many working people to bother to vote for Democratic candidates for national office.

The reader will object that this is too harsh a verdict —that within the parties, particularly the Democratic, there are progressive individuals who want to make the parties, the government, and even (in some indirect way) the corporations themselves responsible to the people. These individuals are the liberals.

It is true that the liberals pose a crucial test of our thesis about the role of elite campaign financing in the established electoral system. We shall therefore focus, in the balance of the book, on the nature of the political philosophies and the fiscal constituencies of liberals.

5

FINANCING LIBERALISM

The role of the rich in political finance entails the willingness of candidates to limit their political positions so as to protect the corporate power structure. Nowhere is this fact clearer than in the "left" reaches of American electoral politics. The most liberal politicians in America are not funded in different ways from their moderate, conservative, and reactionary brethren. There is a democratic funding alternative, however, and it is useful to visualize it, if only to throw into relief the realities of the financing of national electoral liberalism.

A DEMOCRATICALLY FINANCED POLITICS

The democratic alternative to the present systems of campaign fund-raising is neither government funding of parties nor the increased use of computerized, Madison Avenue—managed mail drives (both of which have often been stressed by liberal-minded critics of election funding). Rather, the democratic alternative is dues financing (supplemented by collections at political meetings).

Under a system of dues financing, people who have been won over to the political program of the party pledge to support the party over time. The party derives most of its funds from these dues-paying members and is thereby encouraged to be responsible to its supporters. To raise very much money by means of a large number of persons paying modest dues means that the political party would have to be seen by many working people as genuinely important in advancing their interests.

A dues-financed political party would have to be cohesive and coherent enough that its leaders and governmental office-holders (if any) actually stood politically for the party program. The party might, in addition, provide social services for its members. Without a cohesive, programmatic party, people would have little incentive to contribute regularly to the party as such.

Even if America had cohesive parties with principled loyalty of the elected office-holders to the elected party leadership and to the party program, and with central financing—common attributes of disciplined organizations worthy of the name "political parties" —huge amounts of money might still be spent; after all, costs in Western Europe's and Great Britain's more centralized party battles are not low.[1] But our chaotic politics of multiple and transient private campaign organizations operating under the Republican and Democratic labels makes it impossible for funding to be put on a democratic basis, relying as it does on many small dues-payers supporting a national party program. Since parties do not govern, do not stand for distinctive governmental programs, and do not fund their own candidates, it is difficult for many people to develop deep financial commitments to them.

Even the existence of programmatic, cohesive parties financed by the people would not necessarily mean a democratic politics antagonistic to the interests of the class that now rules through government and corporations. A democratic politics does indeed require a programmatic party financed by the people; but it also requires a party substantively committed to the substitution of democracy for the existing power structure.* Democratic financing is a necessary but not sufficient condition for democratic political struggle.

The idealized dues-financing alternative highlights the shallow popular base of the nonprogrammatic, decentralized "parties" of the U.S. system. All of 1968's campaign costs could have been met had each employed person in the society given $4 to politics.**

* See Chapter Six: The Excluded Alternative.

** If the 76 million civilian employed workers of 1968 had given $4 each, the total fund would have been $304 million.

Responsive parties with genuine popular identification could easily meet even such high political costs as those of today's high-pressure advertising campaigns, and do so entirely without the corporate input.

There was a political party in American history, interestingly enough, that was cohesive, programmatic, and known to have financed its political activities largely from dues. It was the very small Socialist party of pre–World War II days.[2] Party members paid small monthly dues, and money raised in this way was supplemented by collections at meetings, tickets for social events, extra contributions, and assessments of the modest number of elected Socialist office-holders.[3] The number of dues-paying members was, however, much smaller than the number of people who voted for the party's candidates. (Socialist votes nationally exceeded 900,000 in 1912, 1920, and 1932.) [4] But in the same period, socialist parties in other countries were getting much bigger dues bases; before Hitler outlawed it, the Social Democratic party of Germany was getting a minimum of 25 million dues-paying members annually.[5]

This is not to suggest that socialist parties here (or even in countries where they had more electoral success) had effective democratic strategies. The Socialist party itself was eclipsed in the general decline of the left, though it still exists. The American left was first co-opted as the New Deal articulated (but did not implement) goals of economic justice, and was later repressed in the anticommunist program after World War II. But the financing methods of the socialists provided an instructive contrast with the two major parties, which, then as now, depended heavily upon the big contributors.

Liberal politicians in America operate within the framework of the two nonprogrammatic, prosystem nonparties, particularly the Democratic. Consequently there is no dues pool at their disposal and they cannot, operating as individual personalities, realize long-range democratic methods of finance, for these require *party*-supporting income.

THE FUNCTION OF LIBERALISM

At least since the era of Franklin D. Roosevelt, most people anxious for the realization of a democratic society have looked to liberal Democrats as a viable source of change—initially, as agents of domestic social justice; more recently, even as agents of a nonimperial foreign policy. As we have seen, distributive justice at home and a pacific foreign policy would both strike directly at corporate powers, privileges, and programs. Yet the prominent liberals who have articulated progressive goals have not seriously challenged the class power structure or even the ideological cloak of American imperialism.

The case of Eugene McCarthy illustrates the accommodative function that the liberal insurgents perform. As the war in Vietnam continued in 1967 and 1968, the antiwar movement intensified. Bigger and bigger crowds demonstrated in the cities. Not only did organized resistance to the draft grow, but within the army itself the GI's were identifying with the peace movement and were beginning to rebel—to go AWOL, to resist orders, and to make surreptitious armed attacks on officers. The racist overtones of the war against Vietnam were, moreover, a contributing factor in the rebellions of urban black workers. Dissent and discontent threatened to get out of hand—to break out of the law-abiding bounds within which the rather moderate antiwar organizations tried to contain it, and to become the sort of generalized mass unrest that could inspire the birth of a serious antigovernment political movement.

In this setting Senator McCarthy announced that he

would challenge President Lyndon Johnson in the Democratic Presidential primaries of 1968. The electoral process had seemed increasingly closed; Johnson's 1964 election landslide at least partly depended on his rejection of Republican candidate Goldwater's seemingly strident militarism, but his subsequent policies revealed what is in fact true of the established electoral process: it offers no real choice and is not a vehicle of popular control of policy.

The citizen's dignity as a person demands that he have some say in the process of his own rule. Otherwise he is a mere subject. When he becomes convinced that he has no say, that he is but a ruled subject, he is much more likely to rebel than when he can retain some hope in his ability to affect the governmental future. In 1968, for many people, McCarthy made this hope possible again. Certainly, the relief and enthusiasm with which many previously alienated students served him as political workers were obvious. McCarthy himself stated often that he saw one of his purposes as restoring faith in the electoral system.

We do not know how well the liberal tycoons who paid for most of McCarthy's enormously expensive 1968 crusade understood that they were doing much more than merely financing the expression of their own disgust at the course of the war. We do know the objective result of the great electoral challenges by McCarthy and, soon afterward, Robert F. Kennedy. They repaired the popular credibility of the electoral process. They created the illusion that electoral challenge had forced Johnson to modify his war policy and that whoever was next elected President would have to proceed to disengage in Vietnam as a result of the increasing unpopularity of the war.

In reality it was only the fact of increasing antiwar discontent (the in-the-streets movement and allied events in ghetto, in army, and on campus) which entered into the calculations of the policy-makers, whose basic policy was little inconvenienced by the minimal objections McCarthy and Kennedy raised in their "antiwar" campaigns.[6] But the McCarthy campaign affected the antiwar movement, which was never the same afterward. The flicker of real resistance to government tyranny gradually and fitfully lapsed, and the war raged on to the writing of this book—but with vicious airpower, instead of the unsuccessful and actually dangerous use of a mass conscript army, as the main weapon. McCarthy's liberal challenge channeled discontent into the system; the tycoons' investment in McCarthy helped to secure the stability of the power system.

FINANCING LIBERALISM

From 1966 on, large amounts of liberal and antiwar money flowed to various Democratic national candidates, Congressional and Presidential, in support of their efforts to reestablish that party's Depression-born credit with many "average" people. Since the liberals of national politics are no more reluctant to mesh their programs with the requirements of the corporate productive system than are the nonliberals, no conflict of interest between the funders and the funded was involved and the liberal members of the corporate rich were quite enthusiastic in their generosity.

A 1972 advertisement in *The New York Times* announcing the formation of a temporary group to funnel money into the delegate selection process for the national conventions (People Politics) read:

Let's remember, 53% of us are women; about 13% of us are blacks, chicanos and other minority group citizens; and 27% of us are between the ages of 18 and 30. Collectively, we represent a very large majority of the electorate. . . .

[W]e, the people can elect our next President and not

just settle for the backroom choices of the party bosses.
That's why People Politics *was formed.*[7]

The author of the signed advertisement was Stewart Rawlings Mott. When Mott wrote the ad his father, Charles, owned millions of dollars' worth of General Motors stock—indeed, he owned more than anyone else and sat on the GM board. Over 30, white, and male, Stewart Mott sat on the boards of directors for several corporations linked to a family fortune of $800 million.[8] In his advertisement he neglected to mention the biggest majority of all, the wage-and-salary employees of the business class; but then he was in the minority on that dimension, too. Despite his ingenuity in identifying himself as an insurgent against the bosses, it is doubtful that Stewart Mott pressed his father to have GM turned over to the workers, or even to have the firm surrender its war contracts (which include antipersonnel weapons systems projects).[9] But Mott has given hundreds of thousands of dollars to liberal politicians.

Mott gave over $200,000 to McCarthy's campaign in 1968.[10] He bankrolled selected liberals in 1970. In 1972 he began to support McCarthy financially, but then gave over $400,000 to McGovern's campaign.[11]

Mott was only one of dozens of givers of $10,000 and over to the McCarthy campaign of 1968. Many of McCarthy's big contributors were from Wall Street. * The millions of dollars provided by big bankrollers to fund the McCarthy drive were not surprising. What was

* McCarthy's belief that it was in the interest of the United States to agree to a coalition government in South Vietnam—that it was wiser to cooperate with the National Liberation Front and North Vietnam than to continue to try to crush them—was a perfect reflection of the tactical discontent over the costs of the Vietnam war among many members of the corporate rich. McCarthy's conception of national interests and of wise policy in no way challenged the fundamental assumptions of the foreign policy the elite have formulated in their own behalf for decades. In short, McCarthy was no anti-imperialist, let alone anticapitalist, and his generous backers understood that.

surprising was the McCarthy campaign's reputation as a popular insurgency. In fact, McCarthy did not move until he was sure that a substantial campaign chest was there. Big early money was the prerequisite for a serious campaign.

The narrow limits within which liberals formulate proposals for change make it possible for many big givers to shift from liberals to other types of candidates and vice versa. J. Irwin Miller, for example, is a well-known Republican bankroller. In 1968 he was head of the Rockefeller for President Committee. He gave regularly to national GOP party committees that were not tied to any specific candidate. Miller is the chairman of the board of the Cummins Engine Company, an Indiana firm that is among the top industrial corporations in the country. He is also a director of giant Chemical Bank of New York and a stockholder and director of the biggest utility (American Telephone and Telegraph), among other business interests.

Miller has the typical elite "nonbusiness" interests. Besides presiding over the smallish Irwin-Sweeney-Miller Foundation (1969 assets: $26 million), he is a trustee of the Ford Foundation (1970 assets: $2.9 billion). His interest in election financing extends to the Citizens' Research Foundation, of which he is a trustee. In short, Miller's multiple corporate positions and his complementary charitable and civic interests are those of a characteristic mainline Republican member of the ruling class. But Miller is also a financier of liberalism. In 1972 he provided $225,000 for liberal New York mayor John Lindsay's campaign for the Democratic Presidential nomination. Miller also gave $16,000 to the brief antiwar, anti-Nixon campaign of California Congressman Pete McCloskey.[12]

McGOVERN

In 1972, George McGovern was the serious liberal insurgent in the race for the Democratic nomination.

With the aid of a superb private campaign organization and with the help of party reform rules he knew well (having chaired the commission that wrote them), he gathered enough delegates to win. In the preconvention part of his campaign he was somewhat critical of a governmental and economic process dominated by the corporate rich, and he proposed tax reforms for a modest redistribution of income. Perhaps it was his sidling up to the politics of economic justice— something that had not been done for a generation— that earned McGovern his "radical" label. But in any event, there actually was no question of basic change. Said McGovern:

> The strength of the American economy is due mainly to the dynamic growth of the private sector led by corporations and other businesses. It is sound public policy to create the conditions for business to function effectively.[13]

Not only did McGovern fail to note that the strength of the American economy is based on the productive labor of its wage and salary workers, but in addition he had no quarrel either with the concentrated power of the corporate system or with government policies supportive of it.

As one of the two parties of business, the Democrats naturally enough appoint businessmen as treasurers of the Democratic National Committee. The purpose is to facilitate fund-raising from among the party's most important clientele group—the corporate elite. The influence of the McGovern forces in 1972 made no political difference in the pattern. To succeed businessman and big contributor Robert Short, Donald S. Petrie was appointed treasurer.

Petrie is a former partner in Lazard Frères and Company, a Wall Street investment house identified by Domhoff as one of the key firms at the center of the "Jewish/cowboy" interest group in the corporate economy.[14] Petrie was a member of Lazard Frères from 1967 until he took a leave of absence to raise money for Edmund S. Muskie, the middle-of-the-road frontrunner for the 1972 Democratic nomination. When Muskie withdrew, Petrie immediately went to work for McGovern.

After graduating from the University of Chicago Law School Petrie specialized in corporate law. Eventually he became chairman of Avis Rent-a-Car, whose sale to the International Telephone and Telegraph conglomerate made Petrie a millionaire. He developed multiple business interests, spending two years as a stockholder and director of the RCA Corporation.[15] He also was president of the Peace Corps Volunteers Fund and a trustee of the Rosewater Foundation.

Petrie was a big giver as well as a fund-raiser. His philosophy of political participation was expressed in 1972: "I consider it at least as important as any other charity. It's my form of tithing." [16]

Treasurer Petrie's comparison of politics with charity and religion was apt indeed, since all three organized activities are conservative forces maintaining the power structure.* Nor would Petrie or the other big financiers of liberalism have politics be otherwise. Max Palevsky, an early supplier of big money for George McGovern, was relatively explicit in explaining his

* Charity is for the rich an almost obligatory activity that can give some hope to the wretched of the society, who are viewed as merely unfortunate individuals rather than as the inevitable by-products of class control of access to the means of production and distribution of goods. There is a return to the rich from their charitable activities (over and above tax benefits), but it is hard to tally by the methods of double-entry bookkeeping. Popular acceptance of charity constitutes implied acceptance of the legitimacy of great wealth. The hopes of the recipients focus on the largesse of their ultimate exploiters even as the charitable rich experience moral relief through giving. Like charity, established politics pins the hopes of the people on the ruling class and its representatives and, like charity, it is indispensable in the maintenance of the status quo.

backing for a man he hoped could help to ameliorate incipient class conflict in America. "If this society gets torn apart," Palevsky perceptively observed, "it won't help me or my kids to be rich." [17] In a torn-apart society, in fact, the wealth of the Palevskys might be quite insufficient to perpetuate the wealth of the Palevskys. But in 1972 it could help to save the system from a possible crisis, to ease social tensions but not to abolish class rule. It could do so by backing liberal McGovern.

Palevsky is a rich West Coast Jewish liberal of the type that supplies an important chunk of Democratic party cash. He had spent $50,000 financing Democratic politicians in 1970 and gave over $100,000 in start-up money for the McGovern campaign for the Presidential nomination.[18] A director at the time of the giant Xerox Corporation (among other firms), Palevsky had gotten something approaching $50 million worth of Xerox stock when he sold his Scientific Data Systems to the bigger company.[19]

Palevsky got much press publicity as a big McGovern backer, but he was only one of very many such backers. In fact, it would have been easy to fill this entire book with nothing more than a list of the members of the corporate rich making big gifts to the McGovern organization in 1972—their contributions, their corporate interests, their positions in opinion-shaping foundations, associations, and universities. McGovern, like the other liberals, relied on the corporate rich to organize his fund drives and to provide a huge and indispensable portion of the campaign chest.

George McGovern was a mixture of principled liberal and unprincipled opportunist. In the 1972 campaign he set out a plausible economic reform plan. It involved a $30 billion reduction in war spending, the replacement of most of the welfare system with a system of flat grants to individuals, a revival of public works jobs, and, most crucially, a plan to increase taxes on the rich through a series of reforms in personal, inheritance, and corporate taxes. As solidly within the framework of liberalism as these proposals were, many businessmen were unconvinced that the social crisis was yet so critical as to require conservative reform.

John Loeb, a senior partner in one of Domhoff's major "Jewish Wall Street" firms (Loeb, Rhodes and Company) was one of several long-time big Democratic funders disenchanted with McGovern; he said, "His economic policies bother me." [20] Another distressed funder was a Los Angeles tycoon who had given Humphrey's campaign for the 1972 nomination $100,000; "I am in enormous disagreement with his economic policies," he said of McGovern.[21]

The distress of many big businessmen, even in the liberal wing of the elite, was obvious, so McGovern decided to speak to Wall Street by making a major address on his economic reform plan to the New York Society of Security Analysts. Here the candidate argued that the social crisis *did* require conservative reform:

What is good for business is a balanced economy and a people confident of the essential decency of their leaders, and in this case what is good for business is good for the country. . . .

You cannot justify to him [the worker] the fact that there are millionaires who pay little or no taxes at all, the fact that Standard Oil pays a lower percentage of its income in taxes than he does, the fact that many of the wealthy enjoy tax preferences most Americans cannot share, and it is those facts that have fueled the fires of frustration and discontent across this land. And if we reject prudent, carefully structured tax justice now, very radical tax changes may be forced on us later.[22]

McGovern was correct in identifying the sense of economic injustice as a major source of generalized social resentment. In fact, economic discontent consti-

tuted the only major area of general political agreement between most George Wallace supporters and
most early McGovern supporters.[23] But the reduction in
Democratic giving from among the elite which had
forced McGovern to make his Wall Street speech was
not fully reversed by his argument that the discontent
was so deep as to require some "carefully structured"
income redistribution.

McGovern dropped his original plan to replace the
welfare system with a negative income tax, and he
stopped speaking explicitly of redistribution, but his
opportunistic concessions to the business elite (and
the old-line Democratic party leaders) did not extend
to dropping the promise of "prudent" tax reform, nor
did they need to. The candidate just went out of his way
to make explicit his commitment to the health and pros-
perity of contemporary capitalism. This commitment to
the power structure was inherent in his liberalism anyway. There is little basis for believing that, in the conflict between sentiments of distributive justice and the
commitment to a prospering economic dictatorship
that McGovern would inevitably have experienced as
President, he would have made any consequential
headway in the direction of social democracy.

McGOVERN'S MASS FINANCIAL BASE

McGovern was the first candidate in many years to try
to make a major issue of campaign funding. From the
beginning his organization claimed to have a mass financial base. McGovern's name was placed under a
fund-raising letter which read in part:

*Never before have so many hundreds of thousands of or-
dinary citizens mailed in contributions to keep a campaign
alive. This unprecedented outpouring of support has already amazed the so-called experts who said . . . I didn't
have a chance. Thanks to the priceless support of our Mil-*

*lion-Member Club of contributors our campaign is growing
daily in strength and excitement.*[24]

In reality the numbers of gifts gotten through the
McGovern mail drive were well within the range previously achieved by Republican committees and the
Wallace movement of 1968. His organization claimed
650,000 to 700,000 givers of from $1 to $500.[25] Many millions were raised through the mail drives, but when the
final figures are in and are broken down, gifts of $100 or
less will have amounted to no more than half the total
McGovern fund of 1972. The success of the mail drives
was unprecedented only for the Democratic party,
which in 1972 began to do what Republican organizations had done for years.

The exact portion of funds provided by the McGovern Million-Member Club (which never did get its million members) is not so significant as the fact that it
could not have existed without such resources as those
provided by the Woonsocket Club, set up by the
McGovern organization for givers of $25,000 and up.
All during the campaign McGovern sought—and got
—gifts and loans of $100,000, $200,000, $300,000, and
more. The candidate met often with the biggest willing
tycoons in this city and that city, and these big inputs
gave the campaign its ability to buy big blocs of time
when they were needed, and even to operate the mail
drives. The mail proceeds were not enough—not
nearly enough.

There can be no "democratic" substitute for the
dues-financed politics of genuine political parties with
real popular roots. The democratic claims made for the
professionally managed mail drives with their bought
lists reveal the shallow base of liberalism in America.
McGovern's ideological and financial dependence on
the corporate elite was as real as that of any other liberal. He did not represent an actual political force op-

posed to the class power structure and the policies necessary to its perpetuation, nor did his candidacy even move American politics in the direction of social justice and democracy. Rather, it performed a traditional function of liberalism: it trapped the energies of many who wanted to see an alternative and progressive politics but who, instead of getting started on the job of building it, went to work for McGovern.

The corporate financiers of liberalism are seldom as prominent as David Rockefeller. But they are solid members of the ruling class; their economic, political, and social interests are immeasurably closer to those of Rockefeller than they are to those of us. They are also politically wiser than we, for they understand that the liberals they fund explicitly made their peace with the corporate power structure long ago, while we have perennial difficulty seeing that democracy and popular security cannot be achieved by corporation-backed, sweet-talking liberals.[26]

UNION OFFICIALDOM

Were we to make the hypothetical assumption, purely for purposes of analysis, that liberal politicians would like to reduce their dependency on the corporate rich, we would find, on further analysis, that organized labor does not constitute a source of genuinely independent money. To be sure, labor money does not come from the corporate rich. Our assertion is based, rather, on the fact that the labor bosses who invest the political funds operate well within the limits of the basic conservative ideology. Indeed, within the fundamental "free-enterprise" ideological framework, labor leaders occupy a narrower band than do politicians and businessmen. Union officialdom is seldom so reactionary or so liberal as the most extreme of the elite themselves.

Labor union political money works to fund prounion conservatism and liberalism and to contain extreme liberalism within the Democratic party. Insofar as the liberal pole involves a desire to scale down seriously the warfare state, to operate a less aggressively interventionist imperial policy, and to make a stab at real redistribution of income, it is anathema to a decreasing but still majority number of leaders of big unions.

Union-related political committees have spent large amounts of money at the national level since 1936. Some of the money goes for "political education," registration, and get-out-the-vote drives; some goes directly to candidates. The amount disbursed by national-level labor committees in 1968, $7.1 million, was, in real dollars, more than four times the amount expended in 1936.[27] In the meantime, the political character of the unions has changed considerably. Aggressive organizing, rank and file militancy, and openness to radicals—making real the possibility of building a labor politics against the corporate power structure—had characterized the early period, particularly in the Congress of Industrial Organizations (CIO unions, not those of the older American Federation of Labor, were the source of the 1936 money).

Today, unions are a conservative force unambiguously supporting the existing power structure. In fact, union officialdom tends to support the capitalist assumption bounding the electoral process more rigidly and unimaginatively than some liberal politicians (like George McGovern). Many big union executives, including conservative George Meany, the AFL-CIO head, were repelled by the McGovern candidacy of 1972.

It had taken until 1952 for modern organized labor to drop its nonpartisan national stance and to endorse a specific Presidential candidate—Adlai Stevenson, the Democratic nominee. Labor edged very reluctantly into politics, but today the AFL-CIO does have a fairly broad-ranging legislative program according to which it can measure the votes and actions of office-holders in deciding whether or not to support them. However, all parts of the conventional liberal program of the national union federation are not equal. If any-thing gets the leaders as a group more upset than criti-cism of America's interventionist foreign policy, it is a domestic assault on the organizational prerogatives of the unions they head. By 1968 the labor federation took the innovative step of endorsing a candidate before the Democratic convention. The two chief anti-Johnson in-surgents of 1968—McCarthy and Kennedy—were in-sufficiently enthusiastic about interventionist imperial-ism in Vietnam (especially in the case of the former) and as protectors of labor's organizational preroga-tives (especially in the case of the latter, who as Attor-ney General in his brother's Cabinet had prosecuted Teamsters Union president James Hoffa); so Hum-phrey was endorsed. All three of the main 1968 con-tenders had compiled prolabor voting records in the Senate, but their records did not carry equal weight.

In 1972 the AFL-CIO stepped back and proclaimed neutrality as many component and nonfederation un-ions worked for McGovern in the Presidential cam-paign. In addition to raising issues of social justice in a vaguely radical way, McGovern had in the past voted against repeal of a provision of federal law permitting states to outlaw union shops.

McGovern had also criticized Nixon's Indochina war policy, though in 1964 he had, along with almost the entire Senate, voted for the Tonkin Gulf Resolution that was used to sanction Johnson's intensification of the war. Most union leaders still specifically defended the government's war policy, even though—as a study of local referenda on the Vietnam war as early as 1966 to 1968 pointed out—"disapproval of the war appeared to be related to working-class rather than high-status characteristics." [28]

Of course the labor leaders have high status and high incomes rather than working-class characteristics, a fact of some importance in assessing their political positions. Instead of channeling discontents of the working people against the corporate power structure within which the great majority of wage and salary employees are powerless objects, labor leaders are an important subelite channeling the frustration of workers into the established economic and electoral process.

Despite variable degrees of enthusiasm about Democratic candidates, the labor subelite remains essentially within the Democratic party. The labor leaders are certainly no more ready than are the corporate rich, at this particular point in history, to encourage a reactionary third party. As the corporate rich virtually refrained from funding the Wallace movement in 1968, so did "labor," which, moreover, devoted considerable organizational resources to fighting Wallace's competing claim to speak for the working man.[29]

In a 1967 speech Senator Russell Long (an unusually frank Congressional friend of the oil industry) estimated:

Most campaign money comes from businessmen. Labor contributions have been greatly exaggerated. It would be my guess that about 95 percent of campaign funds at the congressional level are derived from businessmen.[30]

Long was speaking of Congressional campaigns, where labor spending tends to be highly selective. For all national-level spending a more generous estimate is that union spending is, at the very most, equal to a fifth of the money coming from the big givers.[31]

Unions are forbidden by law to contribute to national politics with dues money. There have been con-

117

victions; in 1972, for example, the president of the United Mine Workers of America was briefly jailed following conviction for the direct expenditure of almost $50,000 from union funds (of which $30,000 had gone directly to the 1968 Democratic Presidential campaign).[32] But it is generally unnecessary for union officials to violate the law, for the supply of money they spend politically is derived largely from very small regular contributions by union members to the political funds. The largest single spender is the Committee on Political Education of the AFL-CIO, but many individual unions also spend substantially. Union cadres of course press workers to contribute, and then, in many cases, employers will deduct regular gifts from paychecks.*

The fact that the electoral spending of the corporate rich exceeds that of the labor leaders, on the Democratic as well as the Republican side, is not so important as the fact that union spending is not in any fundamental sense a balance against the spending of the elite. Union officialdom, while not of the ruling class, as a whole supports the class system (irrespective of its subjective self-perceptions). When union members pass on money to the central political funds, they contribute to the process of their own domination.** If this seems paradoxical, the paradox springs from the structure of American society.

---

* Corporations also assist the union heads in maintaining their organizations by deducting dues; most dues are collected through checkoff provisions.

** There is a difference between the union member giving money —or the analogous situation of an average nonunion person making a direct political contribution to the established parties—on the one hand, and the leadership of the unions investing political funds, on the other. While both the leaders and the led are supporting the power structure through giving irrespective of their subjective intentions, it is the union leaders who have the big vested stakes in the existing structure of privileges, and it is the leaders who actively

The most liberal individual politicians within the major parties are no more willing to break with the basic commitment to private big property than is union officialdom, but their interpretation of a fair free enterprise system can lead the more extreme liberals to articulate reforms that go beyond the tolerance of the labor bureaucrats. Thus, the most liberal politicians actually find the corporate rich a more fruitful source of eager givers than the labor organizations.

What accounts for the fundamentally conservative role unions now play in electoral politics? Perhaps the simplest explanation is that which was advanced by Grant McConnell at the conclusion of a historical analysis of labor and politics: "[L]abor has been willing to act in national politics, but most of its political involvement is directed to the goal of organizational security." [33]

On the other hand, it may be necessary to add that for today's labor leaders, organizational (and therefore, personal) security is to be sought within the framework of the economic and governmental process that is the structural source of the insecurity of the working man and of the privileged security of the upper class.

shape the character of the labor movement's responses to government, in the process propagandizing and pressuring the rank and file in a variety of manipulative ways. On the political relationship between unions and the corporate system, see Chapter Two: The Ruling Class.

6

THE EXCLUDED ALTERNATIVE

The alternative that is not advanced in American electoral politics, partly because it will not be financially underwritten by the big contributors, is the one that would abolish the ruling class and its policies and privileges by restructuring the socioeconomic system. This alternative vision recognizes that democracy cannot be achieved by remedying injustices *in* the corporate society, because the corporate society is *itself* a system of irresponsible power—the power (and the privileges) of a relatively very few over the large majority. Corporate control of the economy (and, indirectly, of government) must, by definition, be abolished in order to realize a democratic organization of society.

What, let us ask, would be the situation in a classless *society, a society organized along socialist lines? For society to be "classless" would mean that within society there would be no group (with the exception, perhaps, of temporary delegate bodies, freely elected by the community and subject always to recall) which would exercise, as a group, any special degree of control over access to the instruments of production; and no group receiving, as a group, preferential treatment in distribution. Somewhat more strictly on the latter point: there would be no group receiving by virtue of special economic or social relations preferential treatment in distribution; preferential treatment might be given to certain individuals on the basis of some noneconomic factor— for example, ill persons might receive more medical aid than healthy persons, men doing heavy physical work more food than children . . .—without violating economic classlessness.*[1]

Restructured as a classless society, America would not be without organization; it would be organized in a democratic way. Since no class within the society could control the economy, there would be no classes as we have used the term. There would necessarily be human variety, social differences; but not between rulers and ruled, dominant and subordinate, for the purpose of democracy is to abolish these unjustifiable relationships.

The principles of democracy are not mysterious; it is required only that they be effected. Democratic organization of economy and society would proceed on the basis of some very well-known mechanisms—principally the election of regional, national, and international representatives. Democracy does not preclude the use of executive committees to assist in carrying out industrial and social policy, provided these *are* responsible to representative bodies whose delegates actually *are* "freely elected and subject always to recall," to use a phrase from James Burnham's above-quoted passage.

Burnham called the classless society socialist, but in order to avoid confusion we shall speak precisely of what we have in mind: a democratically organized, classless society, rather than socialism.* The classless or genuinely postcapitalist society cannot simply be one where people make choices in a majoritarian manner, since purely formal democracy could yield new forms of class power and privilege. As Burnham implied, certain substantive requirements have to be included in the definition of the classless society. Existing arbitrary privilege has to be replaced by some general, agreed-on social rule for managing economic life. Consensus on basic rules and norms is at least as important in a developing social democracy as in existing social systems. An increasing majority of the people would need to be agreed on such a guiding princi-

---

* Socialism, as a classical doctrine, aimed at no more—and no less —than such genuine social democracy. But especially in America, socialism has come to connote statist systems (like the Soviet Union, whose leaders fondly, if erroneously, speak of their socialist society) or European-type welfare states. A similar linguistic fate has befallen "communism," which for Karl Marx and Friedrich Engels, authors of *The Communist Manifesto,* denoted a fully achieved classless society.

ple as the elegantly simple and morally appealing classic formula, "From each according to his ability—to each according to his needs." Realization of the principle would constitute the changing and challenging legislative task of a socially democratic America.

The great subversive alternative to established politics is, then, to extend the principles of democracy from the governmental realm (where they are not realized now) to all major areas of social life and to make them effective.

Since the mid-1960's there has been an explosion of political awareness. The ghetto, school, army, and factory rebellions have begun to radicalize the basic political outlooks of many young and some older people—students and workers, whites and blacks, women and men. It has been a long time since such a large minority of people have been so clearly aware of the realities and consequences of the class power structure. The new radicalism is a spark that makes possible a new politics based on the decisive step of explicitly formulating the democratic alternative.

Today, the various submovements of the new radicalism tackle the problem of corporate power from their own special angles. Almost every one of the political manifestations of the new awareness does involve implicit or explicit anticorporate action, but the activists still hold back from taking the key step: forming a political party to express the general, common interest that a vast majority have in a restructured society.

Consequently, the anticorporate activities and projects of the early 1970's have tended to demand that capitalists correct this or that current grievance. If a given strike or struggle is successful, a real but limited concession is won—a raise in wages, a black on the board of directors. But the basic powers of the corporate rich remain quite undisturbed and, in consequence, economic security and political self-determination for the majority remain as elusive as ever. The new activists correctly see that particular patterns of social injustice are ultimately reinforced, maintained, or created by the prerogatives of the corporate controllers. The next step is to challenge that corporate control system itself, to take the leap of formulating the democratic alternative.

THE HARRIS CASE

The democratic alternative requires an entirely new political party, for it cannot be effectively formulated by individual politicians within the parties, however "populist" they may be. The case of Fred R. Harris demonstrated that.

Harris declared himself a candidate for the Democratic Presidential nomination in July 1971. The son of an Oklahoma small farmer, Harris went to law school and then into politics in his home state. He was elected to the U.S. Senate in 1964. In Congress he was a popular liberal Senator, voting and debating no further to the left than were men like McCarthy and McGovern. Harris also did fairly conventional, if progressive, non-Senate service. He served as a member of the President's National Advisory Commission on Civil Disorders (which produced the well-known Kerner Report on the ghetto rebellions). During a term as Democratic national chairman he appointed the McGovern Commission (which reformed party delegate selection procedures). In addition, he was cochairman of the Urban Coalition's Commission on the Cities. But as the 1972 election grew near, Harris' views developed in a more radical direction. He characterized his views as "the new populism."

The new populism consists, ideologically, of a working-class-oriented anticorporate appeal that falls short of actual advocacy of a classless postcapitalist society. The new populism is thus much less than the sort of tough populism that could lead to articulating the excluded alternative. But it comes much closer to that alternative than does the warmed-over New Dealism of the vast majority of national liberals.

In the years preceding the 1972 election a small number of new populists had begun to slip into city councils and state legislatures, particularly in university districts. But for important offices the new populists, radical even though not radical enough to articulate the vision of a democratically organized society, have not quite gotten off the ground politically. Harris apparently intended to remedy that situation in organizing his candidacy:

I ran for president because I believe people want—and are entitled to—fundamental change in their lives and in their society. People feel powerless, and they despair of the political process's being able to change because there is too great a concentration of political and economic power in too few hands.[2]

This is the time-honored theme of mainstream progressivism, but one not much heard in recent decades. Harris himself understood how similar his concerns were to those of an earlier era:

Monopoly has been the great forgotten issue in American politics. There was a time early in this century when the executive power of the big corporations was the number one concern of men running for national office. The presidential election of 1912 . . . was fought over different conceptions of the problem of rising corporate power. Since that time . . . the problems caused by the concentration of wealth in America have . . . gotten worse.[3]

During his campaign for the Democratic nomination, Harris introduced an Industrial Concentration Act in the Senate that was designed to dismantle the concentrated peak of the corporate economy, reversing the growth of monopoly. Yet in his remarks introducing the bill, which contained a careful summary of evidence on the increasing degree of corporate concentration, Harris admitted that the conditions his legislation proposed to correct were "already illegal under existing antitrust law," which was unenforced except for "an occasional action against isolated examples of price-fixing and coercive acts." [4]

Senator Harris said his general purpose was to realize "redistribution" and "deconcentration" to yield and "economic democracy." But he at no time proposed to go beyond the limits of industrial capitalism. Speaking before the Platform Committee at the 1972 Democratic Convention, where he proposed tax reforms more redistributive than those the McGovern forces were willing to see written into the party's platform, Harris proposed legislative reconstitution of a mythical entity he labeled "free enterprise":

There are natural market forces which hold down prices and unemployment. The government must step in where they do not work or to hold them within human bounds, but our government increasingly has intervened on the side [of the big] against natural market pressures.[5]

In proposing that "we can be faithful to America's free enterprise tradition and make it work" [6] Harris unmistakably rejected serious criticism of the institution so sacred in the American political tradition—private economic property. Nothing he proposed to achieve "a better distribution of income, wealth and power" [7] would have extended principles of democratic control to the industrial, financial, and commercial corporations that Chomsky has called "the central institutions of the society." [8]

Consequently, even if Harris' reforms could be legislated, private economic wealth and power, with all its political resources, would remain to begin anew its inherent striving toward increased concentration in industry and wealth. Radical as Harris sounded against the relatively orthodox conservatism of established Republican and Democratic politics, the limited reforms he proposed would, if implemented, have given but partial and temporary relief to the consuming and producing public, due to their inherent vulnerability in a privately controlled economy.

Such projections are speculative, of course, since the main fact about Harris is that he was not able to continue his new populist campaign. From the beginning he depended mainly on fat cats to keep his effort going. Indeed, one of the people who approached him first to urge him to run for the Presidential nomination was Herbert A. Allen, Jr. Allen may have been attracted to Harris' emerging populism, but he was no radical. A super-rich Wall Street investment banker, Allen had given $56,000 to the 1968 Democratic campaign—and $1,500 to the Republicans.[9] He was only one of several big contributors who provided the bulk of the Harris organization's campaign money. The several big Harris backers were not so tolerant as Allen of Harris' growing neoprogressivism. They complained as he pressed forward his attack on the tax privileges of the corporate rich. They stopped backing him. In November 1971 his bankrupt campaign came to a halt. By then Allen had provided about a third of the $200,000 costs of the campaign, which ended in debt.[10] The Harris organization had built up, from scratch, a mailing list of 12,000 potential givers, but now there was no money to pay for making and mailing the letters to solicit contributions.[11]

Harris felt that his specific reform proposals were responsible for his cash crunch, and certainly his financial angels complained about them. But in reality his proposed political strategy was more radical than the content of his potential platform alone, for Harris wanted to unite the working majority around their common economic interests relative to the economic elite. Though clearly within the framework of established politics, he was formulating a *class* appeal and, if he had continued to hit hard on that theme, he would have increased popular awareness of the possibility of action against the class power structure:

> *Ordinary Americans understand better than do politicians that the real conflict over the distribution of income in our society is not between welfare mothers and auto workers; it is between poor working people and rich people.*[12]

Harris spoke directly of what he called working-class issues and as a logical consequence was the only politician in the Presidential campaign to attack racism (which divides rather than unites the people) in any direct way. The idea of bringing low- and middle-income wage and salary workers together, the opposite of the standard political tactic of exploiting and intensifying racial and ethnic and marginal economic differences, was the most radical aspect of the Harris strategy.

Harris was getting a good response from working-class audiences.[13] But his campaign had a long way to go and did not get off the ground. In his withdrawal statement Harris said he could not support other candidates, for none were saying the same thing as he.* Indeed, they were not. (George McGovern, who did succeed in getting ample elite financing, moved further and further from the pseudo-radical economic demands that might have brought him victory, finally claiming that the purely symptomatic problem of "crime in the streets" was the most important issue in the campaign.)

Harris was taken out of the Presidential race in the Democratic party. Financing imperatives directly ex-

* Later he did endorse candidate McGovern.

clude even partial articulation of the democratic alternative within the context of the established national parties. This much the Harris case shows with unusual clarity.

But Harris was not taken out of politics. Had Fred Harris been a tough populist, instead of a new populist, he could have chosen to continue outside the framework of the Democratic party. He could have joined with others in founding an essentially anticapitalist party based on dues and small collections. He could have raised the unraisable issue of the class structure in clear-cut terms. He and others allied with him could have been the ones to step into the developing political vacuum in which fester the unarticulated discontents of so many American people. He could have been one of those founding a serious new politics.

But it would have been the beginning of a long struggle, and Harris was still a careerist. That is, he thought in terms of a serious race for the Democratic party's Presidential nomination as an alternative to building a long-range political movement.[14] Unwilling to abandon his commitment to the central sacred cow of the prevailing ideology—the institution of private (and overwhelmingly corporate) economic property—Harris was pursuing an individual career.

THE NEW POLITICS

Careerism precludes serious radicalism. The democratic social alternative cannot be articulated by a person interested in individual advancement within governmental institutions. Election funding by the rich is but one of several influences that today make it virtually impossible for a person to challenge the class power system by seeking office. It really is true that political careers sooner or later entail a sellout, as many bright young men and women who want to serve the people, but suspect politics, understand (or at least sense). The political recruitment process is not ideologically neutral. Acceptance of the corporate power structure as such is an effective prerequisite for one who wishes to attain office and "responsibly" discharge the present duties of established offices in America. This is an area where election financing has its most subtle and important impact. It reinforces the ideological prerequisites of political careerism.

Since the imperatives that limit the politics of the individual careerist are so evident, we can conclude that principled anticorporate politics and individualism are mutually exclusive political paths. The new politics will have to entail the formation of a political party that is cohesive, principled, and democratically structured —and which rejects the appealing calculus of victory for individual party members at the polls. Indeed, the whole question of whether the existing electoral process is not so closed as to justify virtually ignoring it in building popular support will have to be left open. The new politics, as it may be organized in the mid- to late-1970's, will be staffed by politically concerned people who accept the primary necessity of collective and principled political struggle.

Collective discussion and principled decisions are salient themes in the disparate sects of today's new radicalism. But the step of founding a political party, a seriously-interested-in-winning political party, has not yet been taken. There are a few small socialist parties committed to popular revolution for a classless society, but so far most of the activists who believe the system of class rule unjustifiable have held back from joining one of these parties and working to build its popular base, or from forming the new party that is probably required. For some who are committed socialists, the sectarian debate that plagues the American left is an obstacle to effective action. For a perhaps larger number of new activists, there is a reluctance to make the necessary substantial break with the American political tradition, a break that requires a specific rejection of the free enterprise ideology and a specific rejection of the Democratic party as an agency worth supporting in the hope for partial relief from what is really a very basic disease.

If the new activists in shops and schools can unite and become organized, they can launch the new politics in the 1970's. Of the numerous obstacles that will immediately confront the new politics—it will be attacked by institutions whose requirements and authorities are meshed with the interests of the corporate rich, by big business, labor, religion, mass media, and national government, all speaking essentially as one —the most serious is the prevalence of anticommunism in the American political culture. Anticommunist indoctrination is part of the normal political socialization in this society. It matters little whether the new politics scrupulously avoids describing itself as socialist or communist, even though in their classical meanings these words denote precisely the democratic alternative, for anticommunism labels all radically different economic arrangements from those now prevailing as socialistic or communistic. Underlying anticommunism is the idea that anyone who advocates radically different social arrangements either is serving his own power interests or is unwittingly paving the way for a new ruling class. This idea appears in two main forms.

One of the two types of anticommunism in the political culture is what Frank Parkin has called the "dominant value system." [15] This value system, which we have called the main variant of the prevailing ideology, explicitly endorses existing inequality. Insofar as the working population accepts this form of anticommunism, it defers to and/or aspires to ascend the structure of privileges. Happy democracy, competitive industry, equal opportunity—we all know the myths well.

There is a second main form of cultural anticommunism. It is a sort of backup variant of the prevailing ideology, accommodating unpleasant facts that the first level denies. This, which Parkin has called "the subordinate value system," does not accept the main myths but at the same time rejects the possibility of doing anything about the structure of inequality. It is, in Parkin's words, "a moral framework which promotes *accommodative* responses to the facts of inequality." [16]

The dominant value system, or ideology, is easy to combat, and most activists concentrate their fire on it. But the subordinate value system is actually more important to fight, not only because it is most frequently found among the culturally alienated, but also because it denies the very possibility of the democratic order (which the dominant myth partly accepts). The assumption is that human nature is inherently competitive and aggressive: everybody's out for himself, only the rich got there first, and there's nothing anyone can do except try to get by individually or, at most, try to organize to protect parochial interests within the tolerated structure of privileges.

In reality, human nature is something which, within biological limits, develops historically—and it is not basically "territorial" or "aggressive." [17] But cynicism about human nature serves the system well, and to combat it the new politics will have to do more than just point to systemic patterns of injustice. The new politics will have to do more than merely reject statist totalitarianism in an unequivocal and unmistakable way. It will have to positively *affirm* the necessity of a classless society.

A classless society simply is one in which no group within society controls the economy that is the basis of the lives of all. Unless the actual possibility of such a democratically organized order is vigorously pointed out, the cynical root of anticommunism will remain untouched.

The new party will have to publish a newspaper with reports of popular struggles in order to relieve the people of dependence on the procorporate media.

Even more is required. The initiators of the new politics movement will have to involve themselves in concrete local and national struggles of small groups of working people against specific injustices. Through serious involvement in popular activism the party can win people to join it and can involve them in its internal governance, in the process helping to build popular political self-confidence. If, on the other hand, the new politics makes the mistake of lecturing abstract dogma, of judging the people on whether or not they immediately break out of the deeply rooted attitudes of the subordinate value system, it will be decisively and properly rejected. It goes without saying, finally, that while a lot of money will be spent to crush a serious new politics, the party will not (and should not) have financial backing from among the corporate rich.

The vast majority of people in this society (as in others) have a common interest in joining together in a new political party through which they can realize control of their lives. This majority is the working population. The working class consists simply of the wage and salary, white collar and blue collar, employed and unemployed workers in the society.

However, employees who have been given supervisory (managerial, administrative, police) responsibilities will have privileges and loyalties binding them very closely to the powers that be. Few will be won over to the new politics under even the most favorable of circumstances. The small business class, too, is suspended between the ruling class and the working class. These profit-makers are increasingly subordinate to the corporate rich, but they will not identify with a democratic movement designed to liquidate business as we know it. The new politics may articulate its principles in universalistic language, but few managers or businessmen, large or small, will be attracted to it.

The dominant value system is now visibly eroding, much to the concern of the elite and the nonpartisan partisans of the established order. The two major parties mean less and less to the people, who increasingly realize that the real issues, whatever they are, are not those articulated by Democrats and Republicans. The parties will persist organizationally, if only because they share a semiofficial monopoly on the governmental offices. But as entities with electoral support they are disintegrating. Only 54 percent of the eligible voters cast ballots in the Presidential election of 1972. In a sense, therefore, the real results of that election were:

Choice	Percent*
No candidate	46
Nixon	33
McGovern	21
Others	1

More than mere apathetic nonparticipation is involved here. A Harris poll taken in 1967 found 64 percent of the respondents agreeing that "only a few men in politics are dedicated public servants" and 54 percent agreeing that "most people are in politics to make money for themselves." [18] There is a growing disaffection from the electoral system as such against a backdrop of real social ferment.

Women clerical workers striking against the United Auto Workers Union leadership, previously quiescent public school teachers (including professors!) organizing and striking, even homosexuals organizing publicly are just a few examples of the real boldness of a significant section of the working people. There is also

* Figures do not add to 100 due to rounding.

a reactionary backlash against the new boldness, particularly against black militancy. Backlash provides the basis for a possible rightist antigovernment politics (fascism). Since unrest is going to continue, backlash is going to continue. The reality of backlash is just another reason for partisans of a democratic way of life to speed the new politics into reality.

Whatever one's personal, "normative" preferences, the value crisis of the 1970's exists. In many people political disaffection takes the form of a drift away from the dominant value system toward the subordinate system (not to a democratic or egalitarian attitude). Even so, the ideological volatility produced by the erosion of happy confidence in the authorities and the system makes the possiblity of a new politics more real than in four decades. Because the crisis in political confidence can create the opportunity for a serious radical politics, its mere existence is a cause of concern among the many intellectual, political, and corporate spokesmen for the class power structure, who increasingly urge reforms to counter popular disaffection.

7

reforms (again)

REFORMS (AGAIN)

THE CRISIS OF CONFIDENCE

*There is evidence of growing alienation on the part of
the American public from their political and governmental institutions. It is imperative that any such tendency be checked and reversed. Adoption of the measures here proposed would increase constructive
citizen participation in public affairs, enhance public
confidence in the probity of elected officials, and
strengthen faith in . . . our representative democracy.*
Above all, *they would serve to create the foundations
for a more stable and law-abiding social order.*—
Financing a Better Election System (New York: Committee for Economic Development, 1968), p. 26.
(Emphasis added.)

The American elite detect, even more clearly than
do many of us, the crisis of political confidence in
America. The legitimacy of authority in this society is
threatened and this, "above all," dictates reform. In the
case of the passage quoted above, the reforms proposed were directed at the election financing system in
America.

The organization sounding the alarm and formulating the proposals was the Committee for Economic Development, a policy-formulation group. It consists of
almost 200 of the corporate rich (plus a few university
administrators). It represents the less reactionary segment of the ruling class. The CED has authored dozens
of reformist reports dealing with almost every current
issue. In every case the purpose of the CED, which includes many of the relative liberals of the big business
world, has been conservative. CED's general statement of its purposes concludes:

*CED believes that by enabling businessmen to demon-
strate constructively their concern for the general welfare, it
is helping business to earn and maintain the national and*

*community respect essential to the successful functioning
of the free enterprise capitalist system.*[1]

This purpose, described as "nonprofit, nonpartisan, and nonpolitical," is of course the opposite: partisan and political, and aimed at protecting the profit system of the corporate rich as a class. CED's purposes are class-wide rather than factional; the term "nonpartisan" connotes an effort to support the system of authority as such (rather than to advance some particular interest within the system). It matters little whether the Committee for Economic Development really believes that the corporate system is free and the governmental system democratic; what matters is that the group is explicitly committed to preserving a system which is, in actual fact, undemocratically unfree.

The conservative purpose of the CED was also reflected in a 1970 report on Congress. Again, the crisis of confidence:

There is no doubt that there has been an erosion of popular support for Congress. This is injurious to the nation as well as to Congress. . . . Prompt action on several fronts is needed to restore trust.[2]

And, once again, several proposals, including reform in Congressional campaign finance, in order "to improve Congressional operations and to enhance the Congressional image." [3] The reforms were not designed to change patterns of political representation and power, but, admittedly, to rejuvenate popular faith in the system.

The CED is not the only policy body concerned about campaign finance in the context of the crisis of confidence. Another elitist group is the Twentieth Century Fund (founded and endowed after World War I by pioneer business liberal Edward A. Filene). "It is clear," began a 1970 Fund report on Congressional election financing, "that there is something wrong with the nation's electoral system. There are many signs of popular disaffection." [4]

An earlier TCF campaign finance report had argued that "popular suspicion that 'politics is a rich man's game' adds to public cynicism about politics itself." [5] Like the CED (and like other reformers interested in election finance), the Twentieth Century Fund expressed a desire for a republican system functioning more in accordance with its ideals. But the overriding concern, the clincher in the argument for new legislation, is always the confidence problem. "Undoubtedly the weaknesses in our legislation are a main reason for the cynicism about money in politics." [6] If this overstated the actual effects of legislation, it nevertheless made clear the rationale for new laws.

Now, concern about political spending legislation has naturally been a constant concern among politicians. Within Congress, interest in such laws is as perennial as is the low priority assigned to such matters by the powerful within the legislature. Every now and then, though, the reform impulse comes to a head. The policy statements by the Twentieth Century Fund and the CED from 1968 on were indications that this was happening. In addition to the elite groups, many nonelite groups, academic experts, and Congressmen themselves, all concerned about the crisis of confidence, became increasingly serious about reform.

The Congressmen and interest groups who politicked for election finance reform were liberals who shared the same conservative goals as the liberal elite policy bodies, for American liberalism is dedicated to change only in conjunction with conservation of the basic class and institutional structure of this society. Liberal sincerity in desiring a less undemocratic governmental process is not disproof of this fundamental purpose.*

* In the anticommunist crusade of the post—World War II period, the ideological liberals—most importantly those in the labor union

The liberal forces that lobbied in Congress for election reforms (some of which were eventually enacted in 1971) included the AFL-CIO (primarily interested in a scheme to subsidize Presidential elections and in protecting union political spending prerogatives), Common Cause, and, especially, the National Committee for an Effective Congress (NCEC).

Common Cause is a general issue-oriented group that was founded in 1970 by aristocrat John Gardner (former Secretary of Health, Education and Welfare) and a few wealthy supporters, and then enlisted as members those willing to pay $15 a year or more in response to advertisements and mail drives.[7] More liberal than the AFL-CIO, Common Cause continued to monitor conformity with the reform legislation after it was enacted in 1971.

The NCEC was founded in 1948, soon after its antiradical ideological precursor, the Americans for Democratic Action, and concerned itself primarily with financial assistance to selected Congressional candidates.*

leadership and, as Domhoff has shown in the Americans for Democratic Action—led the way to discrediting not only the Communist party but any type of progressive movement outside the framework of the Democratic party. These explicit commitments to capitalism in general and the Democratic party in particular, constants to this day, justify Domhoff's conclusion that "the establishment liberals who lead the way to small social reforms also determine the left limit of what is acceptable opinion within the American polity" (*Fat Cats and Democrats*, p. 142). The national liberals oppose not only the ineffective radicalisms of the present but the very idea of forming an effective independent radicalism for the future. In this, too, they are sincere.

* Some (but not most) of the 30 NCEC members are liberal New York fat cats of election finance like Stewart Mott, Robert B. Gimbel, and Orin Lehman. The NCEC gets money through ideological mail appeals (to which, during a two-year Congress of the late 1960's, some 70,000 contributors responded). Additionally, the NCEC acts "as a middleman between wealthy contributors and needy candidates who represent an antiwar stance on Southeast Asia and hold positive views on . . . domestic issues. . . ." Roger Peabody *et al.*, *To Enact*

In 1969, though, its officers and key members decided to introduce campaign finance legislation in Congress, and NCEC continued to play a key role in the politics of the legislation.[8]

In hearings on the Federal Election Campaign Act of 1971 the NCEC's chairman reminded a Senate sub-committee of "the very serious problem of eroding public confidence in public officials" and made the assertion (with which the Senators did not quarrel) that "the first right . . . of constitutional govern-ment is to preserve that form of government." [9] The NCEC spokesman argued that the bill was good on its merits, but his ultimate emphasis was on the problem of confidence:

The obvious association of money and politics in the pub-lic mind is dangerous, for it undermines confidence in the ability of government to function as a trusted instrument of the people, rather than the tool of a rich few.[10]

Any reactionary tycoon ought to agree with such a statement since it addresses itself not to the justice of the class position of the rich in political society, but rather—and not uncondescendingly—to the state of "the public mind." However, from the public's mental state the NCEC chairman deduced the necessity of re-form. "Reform of the electoral process," echoed NCEC's national director, "is fundamental to repairing this crisis of confidence." [11]

Finally, the politicians in Congress articulated the reform theme. Perhaps they were genuinely concerned with securing "honest and informative election cam-paigns," but they obsessively returned to the problem of "the opinion of the people of the Presidency and Congress, which are both considered to be in disre-

a Law (New York: Praeger, 1972), p. 38. See also Harry M. Scoble, *Ideology and Electoral Action* (San Francisco: Chandler, 1967), pp. 113–115.

142

spect at this time." [12] The cosponsor of the Senate
bill, Mike Gravel, summed up his understanding of
the issue:

*We are at the crossroads. We can either seize the un-
precedented opportunity of revitalizing the political process
. . . or we can consciously allow the dangerous trend of the
alienation of citizens from our political system to gain momentum with every election.*

*The growing disaffection with the electoral process is di-
rectly traceable to our present methods of campaign funding and the widespread misuse of the media.*[13]

There you have it—the conservative purpose of reform.

THE REFORMS OF 1971–1972

In the Congress of 1969–1970 different reform bills were
introduced but only one, limiting expenditures for political broadcasting, was passed by both houses, and
it was vetoed by the President.[14] But reform momentum continued into the next Congress. In 1971,
one major reform proposal was rejected, but others
were passed.

The rejected reform was a plan to subsidize Presidential election campaigns. Taxpayers would be able
to direct $1 of their income tax ($2 on joint returns) to a
government fund, and the money, if forthcoming, would
be dispensed under a complex formula that would have
made over $20 million available for each major cam-
paign of 1972 (Republican and Democratic) plus over
$6 million for any Wallace campaign. The tax subsidy
plan was similar to one enacted in 1966 but repealed
before it became operative.

Democratic Congressional leaders, whose crea-
ture the tax subsidy plan was, argued that it would eliminate the dependence of candidates on great wealth

—a curious position in view of the demonstrable eagerness of Democrats to solicit through and from fat cats, unless one keeps in mind the alienated publics to which such claims were directed. In fact, the ultimately postponed * subsidy scheme involved only the Presidential campaign and, even there, omitted the primaries—where in 1968, more money had been spent than in the general election and where, as Fred Harris found out, the bankrollers of early money have their crucial impact.

Government subsidy remains a goal of some reformers. One liberal academician who chronicled the defects of the 1971 plan nevertheless gave it some credit—"undue influence and the erosion of public confidence in government are diminished," he argued.[15] But neither he nor other prosubsidy reformers would cut out the input of private big money in national politics.

One of the successful reforms was part of the Revenue Act of 1971. It was a tax-credit scheme such as had been proposed by the CED and the Twentieth Century Fund as well as by Congressmen and students of campaign finance. Under the system, taxpayers who give up to $25 to politics at any level ($50 for filers of joint returns) can get a direct tax credit of 50 percent of the amount contributed. Alternatively, up to $50 in contributions ($100 in a joint return) can be deducted from taxable income. The tax credit is designed to stimulate increased popular giving to campaigns, a universally advocated goal among the reformers.

The liberal section of the elite favors reducing the portion of campaign money it provides, but not eliminating its funding role. The CED argued that "costs of

---

* Partly because of Presidential pressure, Congressional leaders altered the subsidy plan to become effective *after* the 1972 election. The overwhelming political likelihood is that, in Nixon's words, "this provision . . . will not become operative." Peabody, *op. cit.*, p. 215.

campaigns should be spread far more widely to strengthen the sense of citizen involvement," [16] a theme echoed by the TCF. "Popular suspicions concerning political finance—and the consequent cynicism—would be allayed if hundreds of thousands or millions of small gifts were to replace a few thousand large donations." [17]

This recommendation is based on the unarticulated and not irrational expectation that broader giving, in itself, will not change the commitment of all major parties and interest groups to the corporate system as a basis for all policy. It is because of this commitment that a contribution by *anyone* to the established parties and lobbies is consistent with and tends to support the system of power we have described in this volume.

The elite have no intention of relinquishing their election finance input. The proposal is only to supplement the corporate input with a visibly increased amount of small gifts to realize "citizen involvement" —to make things look better and to make people feel better about the government. In the long run, and possibly in the not-so-long run, it would be dangerous for the corporate rich to eliminate the direct financial dependency on them of major government office-holders. Virtually no one—not the academic experts who testify before Congress, not the members of Congress, and most certainly not the elite policy formulators— proposes foreclosing campaign giving by the rich. In fact, in the Federal Election Campaign Act of 1971, upper limits on individual campaign gifts, on the books though quite unenforced, were repealed.

The Federal Election Campaign Act (hereinafter called the 1971 Act), which became effective early in 1972, was the most general reformulation of election finance legislation since 1925. Its most heralded provisions were those concerning disclosure of uses and sources of campaign-oriented money.

Curiously, reformers had persistently asserted that publicity about sources of money would itself tend to ameliorate the crisis of confidence. Arguing strongly for full disclosure of sources, the Twentieth Century Fund contended that with secrecy "beliefs about political finance that undermine respect for our political institutions will persist." [18]

The argument that full reporting would pacify the disaffected citizen even when the disclosures reveal even more fully the role of the fat cats of political finance seems to be based on the happy idea that people's suspicions are just unfounded "beliefs." Ideological blinders must prevent the liberal elite reformers from seeing that popular cynicism about the domination of government by big money has an eminently rational basis. Disclosure of more facts is likely to increase, not decrease, popular dissatisfaction. Individual politicians and political financiers, who have regularly shown an appreciation for the virtues of secrecy, have shown a clearer and less ideologically clouded view of the mind of the citizen than the coalition of reformers who carried the day in 1971.

If it is properly enforced, the new law will yield a much more comprehensive view of finance than has been heretofore available. All political committees concerned with candidates for election to federal office and receiving or spending $1,000 or more in a calendar year are covered. All are supposed to appoint treasurers and to keep scrupulous records of the names, occupations, and addresses of each giver of more than $10. They are supposed to periodically disclose their aggregate expenditures and the names, occupations, and addresses of all persons giving a total amount of money or anything of value in excess of $100, and the amount given. Committees must also report names, occupations, and addresses of all persons or firms to whom expenditures of over $100 are made.

Committee reports must be made at short intervals near election time.

Of these publicity requirements the key one is the listing of persons who make contributions to political committees of over $100 per year. The old law's similar requirement did not cover primary and preconvention giving; this had been exempted in 1925. Aside from the extension of reporting coverage back to its pre-1925 scope, the only major change in disclosure requirements was the inclusion of strictly intrastate committees that support federal candidates.

To circumvent the reporting provisions of the 1971 Act while remaining within the letter of the law, a giver would need to make, say, 100 gifts of $100 each to different (but allied) committees to yield a total unreported gift of $10,000. It would require some bookkeeping adjustments, but the parties to campaign financing have previously shown little reluctance to do the necessary bookkeeping when it has been desired to get around inconvenient provisions.

The 1971 Act set limits on broadcasting expenditures.* As the National Association of Broadcasters (the broadcast industry association) had urged, limits were also applied to other communications media. The general formula for all nomination and general election campaigns for federal office was 10 cents per eligible voter, or $50,000, whichever was greater. For the Presi-

* Congressional debates about reform have often raised questions about a provision of federal law that requires broadcasting stations which sell time to one candidate to permit all other candidates for the same office to buy the same amount of time at the same price. This requirement, on the books since 1934, is often called the equal-time provision, but it is really not that, since only the candidates with the required money can buy the equally offered time. Moreover, broadcast media are freed from the provisions in their news coverage of legally qualified candidates. The equal-time provision was not repealed in the 1971 Act. Broadcasters were, however, required to sell candidates time at their lowest effective rates.

dential election of 1972 the formula yielded a limit of $14 per candidate for all communications media. Of the limit, up to 60 percent could be used for radio and television. The limit is automatically increased with rises in the Consumer Price Index. Excluded from coverage were the increasingly utilized computerized letters (used to sell candidates as well as to raise funds), staff salaries, travel, canvassing, opinion polls, etc. The limits in the Act did not prevent 1972 expenditures from setting a new record.

The 1971 Act, finally, set limits on what candidates for office could spend in their own campaigns. The limit for spending by a candidate and his family is $50,000 in Presidential and Vice-Presidential elections, $35,000 in Senatorial races, and $25,000 in campaigns for the House of Representatives. This particular set of provisions was a reaction to the several well-publicized millionaires' races of 1970. If enforced it will compel rich candidates to get money from others, not excluding their fellow tycoons, hardly a decisive political difference from the point of view of the issue of class and power raised in this book. *

When the legislative process was complete, every one of the major provisions of the 1971 reforms was one that had been included in the 1968 report of the CED.[19] In addition, one of the strong negative recommendations of the CED—that there should be no government subsidy of campaigns—prevailed despite support

---

* The above are the major provisions of the 1971 Act. The Act also elegantly restated the long-standing prohibition on direct corporate and union institutional giving to candidates, even while explicitly sanctioning one of the methods that was devised to circumvent the original bans (the setting up of "voluntary" political committees to collect money from organization members). The 1971 Act also explicitly forbade Economic Opportunity Act funds from being used directly or indirectly for electoral activity, another in a series of government moves to make it impossible for what was originally billed as the war on poverty to ever slip into the hands of the poor and their activist supporters.

from among some reformers and many debt-ridden national Democrats for such a subsidy. But this is not to suggest that the CED somehow pulled the strings of the whole legislative process. CED recommendations had been foreshadowed by a 1962 commission appointed by President Kennedy and were echoed in later reports by the Twentieth Century Fund and the New York City Bar Association.[20] It is just that the politicians and reformers who constructed the new legislation all had the same general conservative orientation; all of America's major parties and interest groups are ideologically, financially, and/or personally linked to the elite to some crucially compromising degree. The new legislation of 1971 represented a compromise, the negotiated collective judgment of the nonpartisan partisans of the status quo as to what measures would do as much as necessary and as little as possible toward solving what is in the final analysis a public relations problem.

The provisions of the 1971 Act, and the associated tax credit measure, obviously cannot be expected to have any major impact on patterns and quantities of fund-raising and spending by parties and campaign organizations. The dramatic quality of some of the public debate and 1971—1972 media coverage of election finance reform was at odds with the content of the new legislation. But then, the major political purpose of the reforms is to restore public confidence in government, not to change basic policy.

As we have pointed out, the governmental position of the corporate rich is reflected in national policy outputs.* Not only does major policy aim at protecting the systemic interests of the corporate controllers, but minor policies prove compatible with these interests as well. Election finance policy has to be considered minor. Nevertheless a finance policy that cut the rich

* See Chapter Two: The Ruling Class.

out of political funding (limiting them to very slight personal gifts) would deprive them of a useful means of economic self-maintenance and might tend, in the event of any future drift away from the basic ideology of the status quo, to prove incompatible with their interests. Like all reforms legislated within the existing policy process, the structure of the new laws reveals the purpose of leaving the elite free—in this case, to continue to pursue the instrumental activity of bankrolling would-be nominees for governmental office.

It is likely, however, that the disclosure provisions, instead of strengthening popular support for the regime, will have the reverse effect. In that event, there is an option open to the government. It can simply fail to enforce the publicity requirements, instead allowing loopholes and noncompliance to proliferate.* A policy is not merely a set of legal provisions, but laws and rules as actually applied—a pattern of action, not a legal recipe. And the existing government, not some set of ideal administrators and judges, enforces the law.

THE FUTURE OF REFORM

Since 1904, reformers have actively suggested solutions to the "problem" of big political money in a "democracy." Even Presidents have gotten into the act, as

* The Comptroller General, the accounting officer of Congress, will receive the non-Congressional campaign committee reports. The Secretary of the Senate will get reports from committees and candidates in Senate contests, and the Clerk of the House of Representatives in House contests. Copies of reports go to state capitols. A number of politicians, columnists, and academicians felt that a new, independent elections commission would have enforced reporting requirements better than Congressional officers. But it is unlikely that the structure of agencies receiving reports is the weakest link in the law enforcement chain. In the final analysis the question of enforcement is largely in the hands of the Justice Department, which decides whether or not to prosecute, and how.

when, in 1907, Theodore Roosevelt proposed government subsidies for the parties. But neither the reforms
discussed nor, in particular, the reforms implemented
ever seemed to solve the "problem." [21]

National legislation began with the 1907 prohibition
of contributions by corporations—effective to this day
in shaping the form, not the content, of the corporate
input. By 1925 there was a collection of federal laws on
the books—prohibiting, limiting, and disclosing contributions in various ways. Professor Pollock wrote that
the provisions of the existing legislation did not "make
it worthwhile for anybody to enforce them" [22] and, for
whatever reason, nobody did. Yet the great reform of
1925, the Corrupt Practices Act, basically reorganized
and restated existing election finance law (among other
things), and Pollock held to his conviction that there
was "an immediate need for complete revision of our
laws regulating campaign funds." [23]

That is the fate of the reformer—always to look forward to the next reform, even when celebrating the current ones as steps in the right direction. The "problem"
always remains because the extant class-dominated
government has no interest in cutting off its chief de
facto clients, the corporate rich, from one of their time-
honored means of power.

It is true that in the few years immediately following
the 1925 reform the Senate actually refused to seat two
elected men guilty of a number of indiscretions including expenditures that vastly exceeded the limits set in
the Act (the 1925 Act's spending limits topped out at
$5,000 per House candidate and $25,000 per Senate
candidate). But the Administration never took any actions, and the Senate's commendable vigilance disap-
peared completely without having dented the regular
pattern of abuse that existed from the very inception of
the limits.

The limits game was intensified in 1940. During the

course of Senate debate on the Hatch Act, which was intended to keep civil servants out of party politics, limits on the size of individual contributions ($5,000 per year to national political committees) and total expenditures ($3 million per year per national political committee) were added to the bill in a casual fashion and remained upon its passage.[24] The Hatch limits were, of course, never applied. They were evaded. Where there had previously been one major national political committee per party, several now appeared, none spending over $3 million. Individual givers now gave $5,000 apiece to a series of rapidly multiplying local and national committees set up just to receive their big money. Neither administrative nor judicial branches of government bothered to argue the obvious—that fake multiplication of committees to evade Hatch Act limits was illegal.

There is thus no historical precedent for believing that the 1971 Act will be enforced to any degree inconvenient to the fat cats of finance and their political beneficiaries. As sincere as many of these persons may be when they address themselves to the broad "public policy problems" posed by political finance, the history of reform suggests that they cannot bring themselves to jeopardize effectively elite financing of national elections.

There may be an initial period of enthusiasm about enforcement of the latest reforms. A couple of political committees will be charged with misdemeanors and fined pittances. But the enthusiasm will pass, and the real pattern of political finance will remain, unscathed.

Reform has a bright future. After the passage of the Hatch Act, Congressional legislation was introduced in 1948, 1953, 1955, 1956, 1957, 1960, 1961, 1962, 1963, 1964, 1966, 1967, 1968, and 1970, before the reforms of 1971–1972 actually became law.[25] There will continue to be perennial debates and legislative efforts concerned with "democratizing" finance to alleviate "public cynicism." One is struck by the constancy of themes in the debates over finance throughout the century. The responsible reformers seem always concerned to limit the undemocratic power of wealth in governmental politics, just as no reforms ever quite succeed in doing it. Only a radically new politics can achieve the goal toward which reformers vainly strive, but this politics will democratize more than merely political finance.

ELECTION FINANCE REFORM IN PERSPECTIVE

The problem of popular confidence is linked to much more than money in elections. It is linked to the whole electoral process and to socioeconomic realities generally. The calculus of reform has many fertile fields in which to work its wondrous magic. Henry Ford II recently pointed out how broad the challenges facing reformers really are. Ford, the enormously wealthy Democratic and Republican fat cat, civic leader, philanthropist, society figure, world traveler, government consultant, and, above all, member of the corporate rich, articulated the problem in 1966. "[O]ur nation must move rapidly to solve its social problems and thereby eliminate the conditions that breed anger and frustration and blind rebellion," he said in a speech to the National Association of Purchasing Agents. He condemned all forms of rebellion, including the "far right," but it was clear what form he had in mind as the real peril: "I am concerned about the persistence within some elements in our national political life of the idea that business is the enemy of the people," he admitted.

In a country where business plays so important a role, it will always be a prime target for the demagogue who thrives in a climate of frustration and rebellion. The free enterprise system will not gain the acceptance it needs until all men share in the abundance that system provides.[26]

Ford's position provides the basic rationale for liberal reform—reform aimed not only at public cynicism about campaign finance, but at social despair generally. Reform—designed not to abolish the system of class power and privilege, but to secure it through the appearance of equity, democracy, and justice.

With specific reference to the electoral process, the business liberals have a veritable stable of reforms in wait. They will be trotted out from time to time: a national Presidential primary (abolishing the conventions), a national voter registration system (replacing state systems with their inefficiency and slippage), direct election of the President (abolishing the electoral college), partial subsidies for established parties, and so on. Each reform, like the 18-year-old vote (long a favorite responsible reform project until it was enacted), will promise to "democratize" politics further and none, not even those actually enacted, will really do so.

This is because democracy is not a matter of form. It is a matter of power and substance. Socially real, democratic control of this nation is in fact the excluded alternative of the reform movement.

The alternative to reform is not the status quo. The reform movement is merely one face of the status quo, simply an enlightened conservative enterprise. The alternative to the reform movement is social democracy —real, substantial, economic democracy. The new politics and the reform movement are alternatives; they represent mutually exclusive futures.

CONSEQUENCES OF THE SYSTEM

Lyndon Johnson understood the electoral process as well as any person can ever hope to. In a Detroit speech

in 1964 he spoke fondly of "our own tax paying, profit-sharing, private-enterprise system of government.
. . ." [27] He was later to define democracy as a system in which people get to "choose their leaders." Johnson's formula cut nicely through false textbook dichotomies between economy and polity. His conception was wrong in but one respect: while people do choose their leaders, they do not share in profits.

Popular electoral participation results precisely in choosing leaders—those who will in fact make policy; the authorities, the rulers. But such participation does not affect basic policy, because an interrelated set of political influences preserves the sanctity of the policy process. One of these, operating to assure the loyalty of the individual office-seeker, is election financing. By the "sanctity" of the process we of course refer to the fact that a serious anticapitalist program cannot be articulated through electoral politics at present. It really is a private enterprise system of government.

Most people accept the legitimacy of the government and of the economic structure. Their acceptance is not nominal, but supported by ingrained attitudes. At the same time, most people have serious objections to the unrestrained exercise of corporate power. Contradictory attitudes are present in all people, and this is particularly so with regard to attitudes toward the political power of the corporate rich in society. An increasing minority actively engage in limited struggle against the powers that be, usually breaking the law in the process. But conservative sentiments are still dominant within most people. Even many of the activists struggle against aspects of the system of authority with the hope of receiving justice somewhere else within the same system.

The fear of equality, of self-government, and of democracy are regularly reinforced in the daily functioning of social institutions. The process is complex, and we have been able only to touch on it briefly in this book. One thing, however, is clear. Unless the alternative to the undemocratic society is vigorously pressed in thoughts and actions that reach the people, they have little experiential basis for imagining that there can be a democratically structured society, let alone for joining a new politics.

In this connection, the purpose of this book has been to clear the deck for some unemotional thinking about the role of elections in America. A majority, albeit shrinking, of people cannot pull themselves away from the hope that it *is* possible to affect the basic shape of our social future by casting yet another national ballot. But this hope is largely an unanalyzed belief, essentially an article of faith. The candidates for national office are all committed to corporate power as the basis for policy formulation. Corporate control of the means of production, and the associated structure of basic inequities, is in turn not even subject to electoral forms. Under these circumstances elections cannot change things much. They cannot bring power to the people, which is what all progressive changes in foreign and domestic policy really require.

It is possible that, whether accepting or rejecting the basic power structure, one may want to vote to have some say, however slight, in the details of development of some government program. Certainly a lot of people have made this sort of calculation in the Presidential elections of 1964, 1968, and 1972 with regard to the future of U.S. war policy in Southeast Asia. If one understands how little the framework of a program is affected by which man wins, and if one has a skeptical attitude about the possibility of even marginal influence, there is nothing irrational about this course of action. But if one rejects the power structure, voting must be balanced against the inescapable fact that the spokesmen of the system, the beneficiaries of its inherent injustices, value any scrap of popular sanction. In a word, they *want* us to vote, "for the party of your choice," but above all, to *vote*. Voting does legitimize the powers that be. And it is not a vehicle of popular self-governance. As to the marginal-influence rationale, it is too often just that—the excuse we use to submit to the emotional pull of the polls. I hope this book can help its readers confront these unpleasant realities.

But in the final analysis a mere book cannot go very far toward restoring popular political mental health. Even if a book is effective, relatively few people get to read it. Moreover, *action* (guided by thought) is far more impressive than mere analysis. So, what the elite must really try to suppress is not this or that book, but the organized political movement that will seriously challenge the powers that be.

notes

PREFACE

1 Milton Friedman, *Capitalism and Freedom* (Chicago: The University of Chicago Press, 1962), p. 17.

2 Louise Overacker, *Presidential Campaign Funds* (Boston: Boston University Press, 1946), p. 19.

CHAPTER ONE

1   Committee on Finance, United States Senate, *Political Campaign Financing Proposals* (June 8, 1967), p. 380.
2   Association of the Bar of the City of New York, *Congress and the Public Trust* (New York: Atheneum, 1970), p. 121.
3   Rowland Evans and Robert Novak, "Glenn Is Seen Victor in Ohio," *The Plain Dealer* (April 16, 1970), p. 10 A.
4   *Congressional Quarterly Weekly Report* (August 14, 1970), p. 2061.
5   *Ibid.*
6   *Political Campaign Financing Proposals,* p. 382.
7   From C. Wright Mills' famous elaborated hypothesis *The Power Elite* (New York: Oxford University Press, 1956).
8   Though he felt the corporate rich fell short of fitting the description, Mills defined the ruling class as "an economic class that rules politically." *Ibid.,* p. 277.
9   James K. Pollock, Jr., *Party Campaign Funds* (New York: Alfred A. Knopf, 1926), p. 41.
10 The exception is G. William Domhoff, *Fat Cats and Democrats* (Englewood Cliffs, N.J.: Prentice-Hall, 1972).

CHAPTER TWO

1   James Burnham, *The Managerial Revolution* (New York: The John Day Company, 1941), pp. 59–60.
2   On the increasing majority of people who are employees rather than entrepreneurs, see Ernest Mandel, *Marxist Economic Theory* (New York: Monthly Review Press, 1968), p. 164.
3   See C. Wright Mills, *White Collar* (New York: Oxford University Press, 1951), pp. 54–59.
4   *Ibid.,* p. 50.
5   Adolph A. Berle, Jr., *The Three Faces of Power* (New York: Harcourt, Brace and World, 1967), p. 29.
6   John Kenneth Galbraith, *The New Industrial State* (Boston: Houghton Mifflin, 1967), p. 74. The 200 figure is

also used in Morton Mintz and Jerry S. Cohen, *America, Inc.* (New York: Dial Press, 1971), p. 58.

7 Gabriel Kolko, *Wealth and Power in America* (New York: Praeger, 1962), pp. 57–59.

8 G. William Domhoff, *Who Rules America?* (Englewood Cliffs, N.J.: Prentice-Hall, 1967), pp. 47–49. The increasing role of banks is reviewed in Mintz and Cohen, *op. cit.,* pp. 86–91.

9 Domhoff, *op. cit.,* p. 57.

10 The corporate rich—officers (presidents, senior executives, chairmen), members of the board of directors, and officer-directors—are big stockholders, despite a good deal of facile mythology (among popular economists) about the unimportance of stockholding (and even profit-making) in corporate control. For factual reviews of the relationship between stock ownership and corporate control, see Kolko, *op. cit.,* pp. 60–69, and Michael Tanzer, *The Sick Society* (New York: Holt, Rinehart and Winston, 1970), pp. 7–20.

11 See G. William Domhoff, *The Higher Circles* (New York: Random House, 1970), especially pp. 21–32.

12 See, for example, Robert A. Dahl, *After the Revolution?* (New Haven, Conn.: Yale University Press, 1970), p. 110.

13 Burnham, *op. cit.,* p. 24.

14 C. Wright Mills, *The Power Elite* (New York: Oxford University Press, 1956), p. 273.

15 Gabriel Kolko, *The Triumph of Conservatism* (New York: The Free Press of Glencoe, 1963), p. 287.

16 For a liberal view, see Dahl, *op. cit.,* pp. 115–140; for a radical view, see Mills, *The Power Elite,* pp. 119–125. The contemporary capitalist economy is called oligopolistic by many liberals and monopolistic by most radicals, but the essential idea—concentrated economic power—is the same.

17 On noncompetitive price-setting, see Paul Baran and Paul Sweezy, *Monopoly Capital* (New York: Monthly Review Press, 1966), pp. 57–64.

18 Mills, *The Power Elite,* p. 116.

19 Leon H. Keyserling, *Progress or Poverty* (Washington,

D.C.: Conference on Economic Progress, December 1964), p. 27.

20 Kolko, *Wealth and Power in America,* p. 14.

21 Frank Ackerman, Howard Birnbaum, James Wetzler, and Andrew Zimbalist, "Income Distribution in the United States," *The Review of Radical Political Economics,* 3 (Summer 1971), 22.

22 Median family income, according to U.S. Census data, was $9,870. The average family was just under four persons.

23 According to 1970 U.S. Census data, over half the wives in families earning $15,000 or more were working.

24 On the aged see Michael Harrington, *The Other America* (Baltimore: Penguin Books, 1963), pp. 101–116.

25 Ackerman *et al., op. cit.,* 27–28.

26 *Ibid.,* 25.

27 Domhoff, *Who Rules America?,* pp. 47, 51.

28 See Grant McConnell, *Private Power and American Democracy* (New York: Alfred A. Knopf, 1967), pp. 250–255.

29 Galbraith, *op. cit.,* p. 77.

30 Domhoff, *The Higher Circles,* p. 249.

31 McConnell, *op. cit.,* especially pp. 298–335.

32 See Clark Kerr, "The General Wage Level," in E. White Bakke *et al., Unions, Management, and the Public* (New York: Harcourt, Brace, 1963), pp. 516–526.

33 *The New York Times* (May 12, 1970), p. 8.

34 McConnell, *op. cit.,* pp. 255–280, 306.

35 Michael Parenti, *Trends and Tragedies in American Foreign Policy* (Boston: Little, Brown, 1971), p. 1.

36 *The New York Times* (August 17, 1971), p. 19.

37 While economists freely admit the basic conservative purpose of interventionism, they do not all agree that it will succeed. Conservatives like Milton Friedman are skeptical largely on account of the main technique (government deficit spending), and radicals like Michael Tanzer are skeptical largely on account of inherent contradictions in the economy. See Milton Friedman, *Capitalism and Freedom* (University of Chicago Press, 1962), Ch. 5, and Tanzer, *op. cit.,* Ch. 7.

38 On the failure of the New Deal's redistributive intentions, see Richard Hofstadter, *The American Political Tradition* (New York: Alfred A. Knopf, 1948), pp. 327–338.

39 See the discussion of the New Deal in Thomas R. Dye and L. Harmon Zeigler, *The Irony of Democracy* (Belmont, Calif.: Wadsworth Publishing Company, 1971), pp. 83–86.

40 For example see the letter to the editor by Massachusetts Institute of Technology economists Lester C. Thurow, Edwin Kuh, John Harris, Jagdish Bhagwati, and Harold Freeman, *The New York Times* (September 26, 1971), p. 14.

41 The wage-price spiral view that literally full employment creates inflation through the effect of wages on prices informs economists' advice to government. For a statement of the contradiction between full employment and price stability, see John Kenneth Galbraith, *The Affluent Society* (Boston: Houghton Mifflin, 1958), pp. 224, 245. Ernest Mandel has argued, however, that state spending, especially on war, is the proximate cause of inflation in contemporary capitalism (*op. cit.*, pp. 526–528).

42 Michael Harrington, "Government Should Be the Employer of First Resort," *The New York Times Magazine* (March 26, 1972), p. 44.

43 See, for example, the overview by Mintz and Cohen, *op. cit.*, Ch. 7.

44 Gabriel Kolko, "Power and Capitalism in Twentieth-Century America," in J. David Colfax and Jack L. Roach, eds., *Radical Sociology* (New York: Basic Books, 1971), p. 219.

45 See the compact review of expert testimony on this subject in Estes Kefauver, *In a Few Hands* (Baltimore, Md.: Penguin Books, 1965), pp. 186–239.

46 Friedman, *op. cit.*, p. 132.

47 Richard J. Barber, *The American Corporation* (New York: E. P. Dutton, 1970), p. 173.

48 Friedman, *op. cit.*, p. 120.

49 *The New York Times* (March 3, 1972), p. 28.

50 Reported in the *Congressional Record* (July 19, 1972), p. H 6709.

51 McConnell, *op. cit.,* p. 253.

52 See *The New York Times* (February 29, 1972, and subsequent issues) for the ITT story.

53 E. E. Schattschneider, *The Semisovereign People* (New York: Holt, Rinehart and Winston, 1960), pp. 30–34.

54 Jeanne R. Lowe, *Cities in a Race with Time* (New York: Random House, 1968), pp. 33 and 168–171.

55 *Ibid.,* pp. 235–276.

56 Martin Anderson, *The Federal Bulldozer* (Cambridge, Mass.: MIT Press, 1964), especially pp. 4, 16, and 52–72.

57 Lowe, *op. cit.,* p. 234.

58 *The New York Times* (March 28, 1972), p. 20 (report by Jerry M. Flint).

59 Kenneth Zapp, "Industrialized Housing and Public Policy," *Technology Review* (February 1972), 20–29.

60 Orville Freeman, "Agriculture and Rural Life," in the Democratic Party Booklet *Toward an Age of Greatness* (Washington, D.C.: The State Committees on Voter Education, 1965), p. 85.

61 McConnell, *op. cit.,* pp. 75–80, 230–243.

62 Charles M. Schultze, *The Distribution of Farm Subsidies: Who Gets the Benefits?* (Washington, D.C.: The Brookings Institution, 1971), especially pp. 30, 40.

63 See H. L. Nieburg, *In the Name of Science* (Chicago: Quadrangle Books, 1966).

64 See Barbara Ehrenreich and John Ehrenreich, *The American Health Empire* (New York: Random House, 1970), especially Ch. 12.

65 Willard C. Richan, "The Two Kinds of Social Service in Public Welfare," *Public Welfare,* 27 (October 1969), 307–311.

66 Domhoff, *The Higher Circles,* p. 155.

67 See William A. Williams, *The Tragedy of American Diplomacy* (New York: Dell Publishing Company, 1962).

68 See Harry Magdoff, *The Age of Imperialism* (New York: Monthly Review Press, 1969), pp. 27–66.

69 To give sources here is a bit arbitrarily selective, since

so much pertinent material is available. Nevertheless, on the U.S. interventions against the Soviet revolution, see D. F. Fleming, *The Cold War and Its Origins* (Garden City, N.Y.: Doubleday, 1961), pp. 20–35. On some of the interventions around the world after World War II, see David Horowitz, *The Free World Colossus* (New York: Hill and Wang, 1965), pp. 114–212. There were over 20 military interventions in Latin America between 1898 and 1926 (Williams, *op. cit.*, pp. 149–150). A history focusing only on military interventions, "from the halls of Montezuma to the shores of Tripoli," would be thick and interesting.

70   In Asia in World War II, "in every actual political situation in which it became involved," the United States "always supported conservative reaction," recorded Harold Isaacs in *No Peace for Asia* (Cambridge, Mass.: MIT Press, 1967), pp. 235, 242. The decisions of which Isaacs wrote in 1947 lay the basis for the endless active military involvement in Asia—and, as Isaacs noted, they were quite consistent with prewar imperial policy (pp. 213–234). For an analysis of the general containment of left forces that was central to World War II policy, see Gabriel Kolko, *The Politics of War* (New York: Random House, 1969), especially pp. 31–37 and 594–626.

71   For a brief review of this pattern see Noam Chomsky, *At War with Asia* (New York: Random House, 1970), pp. 13–38.

72   Fleming, *op. cit.*, pp. 477–501.

73   John Gerassi, *The Great Fear in Latin America* (rev. ed.; London: Collier-Macmillan, 1965), pp. 251–304.

74   *Development Assistance to Southeast Asia* (New York: Committee for Economic Development, July 1970), especially pp. 61, 66, and 70.

75   Even in Latin America, where American power has had substantially free reign for so long, these results are clear. See Gerassi, *op. cit.*, pp. 347–387; Williams, *op. cit.*, pp. 177–183; Edward Boorstein, *The Economic Transformation of Cuba* (New York: Monthly Review Press, 1968), pp. 1–16; and André Gunder Frank, *Capi-*

talism and Underdevelopment in Latin America (New York: Monthly Review Press, 1969, pp. 281–318.

76 Magdoff, *op. cit.,* pp. 115–171.

77 *Ibid.,* p. 200

78 See, for example, the review paper on the Indochina war, "The Cost of the War to the American People: How Much? Who Pays?," *The Review of Radical Political Economics,* 2 (August 1970), 1–7.

79 Mills, *The Power Elite,* p. 235.

80 Domhoff, *Who Rules America?,* pp. 97–100.

81 Douglass Cater, *Power in Washington* (New York: Random House, 1964), p. 247. Richard J. Barnet reports similar results from his study of the 400 persons who held the "top national security positions," 1940–1967. See his *The Economy of Death* (New York: Atheneum, 1970), pp. 87–101. Gabriel Kolko found similar results in his study of 234 "foreign policy decision-makers" of 1944–1960. See his *The Roots of American Foreign Policy* (Boston: Beacon Press, 1969), p. 17.

82 Donald R. Matthews, *The Social Background of Political Decision-Makers* (New York: Random House, 1954), p. 24.

83 *Ibid.,* p. 32.

84 Ralph Miliband, *The State in Capitalist Society* (New York: Basic Books, 1969), p. 62.

85 Association of the Bar of the City of New York, *Congress and the Public Trust* (New York: Atheneum, 1970), pp. 48, 52. The most obvious and particularistic conflicts of interest are probably avoided by some of the members of Congress, as well as by people in other branches of the national government. If they hold stocks in a company doing business with their particular committee or agency, for example, these will be converted into cash or held in trust for the duration of office-holding. This does not mean that plenty of special-interest traffic in influence does not occur. It *does* mean that what businessmen in office always retain is a general interest in the soundness of investors' dollars and stocks. David Packard is as good an example as any of the many big businessmen who take leaves of

absence to enter "public service." He and William Hewlett of Hewlett-Packard hold over half the corporation's stock. The stock appreciated by $19 million while Packard served as Deputy Secretary of Defense in the Nixon administration. The gain was given to charity. While in Washington, Packard resigned all connections with the corporation—except, of course, for the stock. The vast stock holdings gave him an inescapable vested economic interest in the well-being of big corporations. Facts about Packard are from *Business Week* (January 29, 1972), 44.

86 See papers nos. 10 and 51 by James Madison in Clinton Rossiter, ed., *The Federalist Papers* (New York: New American Library, 1961).

87 Friedman, *op. cit.,* p. 16.

88 Hans J. Morgenthau, *Politics Among Nations* (New York: Alfred A. Knopf, 1964), p. 29, for "persuasion"; C. Wright Mills, "Comment on Criticism" in G. William Domhoff and Hoyt B. Ballard, *C. Wright Mills and the Power Elite* (Boston: Beacon Press, 1968), p. 242, for "manipulation."

89 For a thorough case study of a revealing FCC decision, see "How to Get into TV," by Victor Rosenblum in Alan F. Westin, *The Uses of Power* (New York: Harcourt, Brace and World, 1962), pp. 173–228.

90 Eighty-six percent of the members of the Writers Guild polled in 1972 had found from personal experience that censorship exists within television; 81 percent replied that TV does not present society truthfully. David W. Rintels, "Censorship on Television," *The New York Times* (March 5, 1972), Sec. 2, p. 3. Useful books by newsmen dealing in part with their difficulties in reporting news include Fred W. Friendly's *Due to Circumstances Beyond Our Control . . .* (New York: Random House, 1967) and Herbert L. Matthews' *A World in Revolution* (New York: Charles Scribner's Sons, 1972).

91 Constance Holden, "TV Violence," *Science* (February 11, 1972), 608.

92 *The New York Times* (February 19, 1972), p. 1.

93 Former *Newsweek* editor Edwin Diamond in a talk to

the Science and Public Policy Studies Group, Chicago, December 29, 1970.

94 Nicholas Wade, "Freedom of Information: Officials Thwart Public Right to Know," *Science* (February 4, 1972), 498–502.

95 Mills, *The Power Elite,* p. 314.

96 Herbert Marcuse, *One-Dimensional Man* (Boston: Beacon Press, 1964), p. 7.

CHAPTER THREE

1 Alexander Heard, *The Costs of Democracy* (Chapel Hill: University of North Carolina Press, 1960), p. 321.

2 Fred R. Harris, "The Frog-Hair Problem," *Harper's Magazine* (May 1972), 14.

3 G. William Domhoff, *Fat Cats and Democrats* (Englewood Cliffs, N.J.: Prentice-Hall, 1972), p. 31.

4 David W. Adamany, *Financing Politics* (Madison, University of Wisconsin Press, 1969), pp. 212–213.

5 See the analysis of enforcement and reporting problems at the state level by David Rosenbloom, "Background Paper," in *Electing Congress: The Financial Dilemma* (New York: Twentieth Century Fund, 1970), pp. 50–55.

6 James K. Pollock, Jr., *Party Campaign Funds* (New York: Alfred A. Knopf, 1926), p. 27.

7 Herbert E. Alexander, *Financing the 1968 Election* (Lexington, Mass.: Heath, 1971), p. 2.

8 The figures for 1912 through 1956 are from Herbert E. Alexander, *Money in Politics* (Washington, D.C.: Public Affairs Press, 1972), p. 79; for 1960, from Alexander's *Financing the 1960 Election* (Princeton, N.J.: Citizens' Research Foundation, 1962), p. 10; for 1964, from Alexander's *Financing the 1964 Election* (Princeton, N.J.: Citizens' Research Foundation, 1966), p. 8; and for 1968, from the same author's *Financing the 1968 Election,* p. 2.

Direct general election expenditures by national political committees in Presidential election years were, according to these sources, as follows (in millions of dollars):

'12	'16	'20	'24	'28	'32	'36	'40
2.9	4.7	6.9	6.4	11.6	5.1	14.1	7.8

'44	'48	'52	'56	'60	'64	'68
7.7	7.8	11.6	12.9	21.5	26.6	48.1

9 The 1968 percentages are from Alexander, *Financing the 1968 Election,* p. 3. The generalization is based on data in the same place; in Heard, *op. cit.,* p. 20; and in two books by Louise Overacker, *Money in Elections* (New York: Macmillan, 1932), p. 73, and *Presidential Campaign Funds* (Boston University Press, 1946), p. 32.

10 Overacker, *Presidential Campaign Funds,* p. 44.

11 Rosenbloom, *op. cit.,* p. 47.

12 Alexander, *Money in Politics,* pp. 24–26.

13 Joseph W. Barr in Committee on Finance, United States Senate, *Political Campaign Financing Proposals* (June 1, 1967), p. 127.

14 Alexander, *Money in Politics,* p. 226.

15 Alexander's principal books are those listed above in Note 8.

16 Alexander, *Financing the 1968 Election,* p. 3; and Rosenbloom, *op. cit.,* p. 47.

17 Alexander, *Financing the 1968 Election,* p. 3.

18 Heard, *op. cit.,* pp. 7–8.

19 David W. Adamany, *Campaign Finance in America* (North Scituate, Mass.: Duxbury Press, 1972), p. 39.

20 Bureau of the Census, U.S. Department of Commerce, *The Statistical Abstract of the United States* (Washington, D.C.: U.S. Government Printing Office, 1971), p. 318.

21 Alexander, *Money in Politics,* pp. 24, 127.

22 *Ibid.*

23 *Dollar Politics* (Washington, D.C.: Congressional Quarterly, 1971), pp. 24, 29.

24 See John S. Saloma, III, and Frederick H. Sontag, *Parties* (New York: Alfred A. Knopf, 1972), pp. 105–106. The

Republicans rely heavily on mail fund drives for inter-election solvency.

25 Stewart Alsop, "Kennedy's Magic Formula," *The Saturday Evening Post* (August 13, 1960), 60.

26 Edward F. Woods, "How Much Did Kennedy Spend on His Campaign?," *St. Louis Post-Dispatch* (August 7, 1960), p. 1 B.

27 William Ebenstein, C. Herman Pritchett, Henry A. Turner, and Dean Mann, *American Democracy in World Perspective* (New York: Harper and Row, 1967), p. 11.

28 Heard, *op. cit.*, p. 335.

29 Alexander, *Financing the 1968 Election,* p. 11.

30 *Ibid.,* pp. 10, 30; and Alexander, *Money in Politics,* p. 65. There are no data available splitting Wallace's costs into pre– and post–American Independent party convention periods. The Wallace organization reported February-to-October costs of almost $7 million, and for the whole campaign spent over $2 million more (*Financing the 1968 Election,* p. 92).

31 Overacker, *Money in Elections,* p. 21.

32 Heard, *op. cit.*, p. 393.

33 Delmer D. Dunn, *Financing Presidential Campaigns* (Washington, D.C.: Brookings Institution, 1972), p. 37. See also Dunn's general discussion of broadcasting, pp. 35–40.

34 Computed from data in Alexander, *Financing the 1968 Election,* pp. 80, 84, and 92.

35 Alexander, *Money in Politics,* p. 256.

36 Total political broadcast costs for 1970 were $74–80 million. These figures were arrived at by taking the results in Federal Communications Commission, *Survey of Political Broadcasting* (Washington, D.C., 1971), adding 15 percent advertising agency commissions to the FCC's listed charges for time only (see Alexander, *Money in Elections,* p. 225), and adding one-fourth to one-third for productions costs.

37 The firsthand report of a man who worked with Fuller and Smith and Ross, the advertising agency handling Richard Nixon's 1968 television campaign, illustrates how public relations norms shape the broadcasting

framework. See Joe McGinnis, *The Selling of the President, 1968* (New York: Trident Press, 1969).

38 "Money to Nominate," *New Republic* (April 14, 1920), 198. Quoted in Overacker, *Money in Elections,* p. 374.

39 David Rosenbloom, ed., *The Political Market-Place* (New York: Quadrangle Books, 1972).

40 See Saloma and Sontag, *op. cit.,* pp. 294–302.

41 Alexander, *Financing the 1968 Election,* p. 113.

42 Alexander, *Financing the 1964 Election,* p. 70.

43 Walter Pincus, "But the Republicans Invented It," *New York* (September 18, 1972), 50.

44 Undated McGovern fund-raising letter received (several times) by the author in October 1972.

45 Alexander, *Money in Politics,* p. 84.

46 *The New York Times* (July 16, 1972), p. 32.

47 *The New York Times* (May 17, 1971), p. 42.

48 Heard, *op. cit.,* p. 261.

49 *Ibid.,* p. 44.

50 Survey Research Center 1968 Election Study (SRC S 523), tape supplied courtesy of Interuniversity Consortium for Political Research. Polls like the SRC survey are based on very small, carefully drawn samples that are designed to constitute a social cross-section of the population. Since there were only 1,557 persons in the 1968 survey, the numbers of respondents in particular categories were often low, giving rise to statistical errors as follows:

Income	Percent Giving	Statistical Error
less than $4,000	3.2	±1.0%
$4,000–5,999	4.5	±1.5%
$6,000–8,999	7.1	±1.4%
$9,000–11,999	7.5	±1.8%
$12,000–24,999	12.1	±2.3%
more than $25,000	30.6	±9.7%

51 Dan H. Fenn, "Business and Politics," *Harvard Business Review* (May–June 1959), 6–10.

52 *Dollar Politics, op. cit.,* p. 32. *Congressional Quarterly* used contribution data compiled by the Citizens' Re-

search Foundation for the 66 Americans *Fortune* magazine estimated to be the very richest in 1968.

53 Alexander, *Money in Politics,* pp. 113–114.

54 *The Wall Street Journal* (September 27, 1972), p. 35. Maurice H. Stans, who resigned as Secretary of Commerce to become Nixon's chief corporate fund-raiser for the 1972 election, had been a director of Fluor Corporation before entering the Cabinet in 1969. The Fluor Corporation pleaded guilty to making a direct $30,000 contribution to the 1964 campaign, and another to the 1966 campaign, as the result of the only major investigation to produce prosecutions of a number of firms for direct giving. See Morton Mintz and Jerry S. Cohen, *America, Inc.* (New York: Dial Press, 1971), p. 191.

55 Alexander, *Financing the 1968 Election,* p. 163.

56 Alexander, *Money in Politics,* p. 226.

57 Alexander, *Financing the 1968 Election,* pp. 159, 164–165. Percentages calculated from Alexander's raw figures.

58 *Ibid.*

59 *Ibid.,* pp. 7–68.

60 These 2 percent of all known givers of $500 and up gave 42 percent of the amount coming from such givers (*ibid.,* p. 167).

61 Herbert E. Alexander and Caroline D. Jones, eds., *Political Contributions of $500 or More in 1968* (Princeton, N.J.: Citizens' Research Foundation, 1971).

62 These givers are only those from the Cleveland metropolitan area who gave to national-level committees and whose names were so recorded in accordance with federal law. The CFR list does not contain the names of big givers to political committees operating only in Ohio. Another limitation of the data is that persons giving less than $500 on several occasions are not included on the list even if the actual total exceeded $500 for the year. Given the incompleteness of the public records on which the list is based, and errors therein, the editors do not claim the list to be complete or error-free. But the CFR list is the most comprehensive published list available.

No one has ever systematically studied the names of all the givers on the CFR (or any other) national lists, and to do so would require more resources than we had. The value of our study lies in examining the backgrounds of all listed givers from the selected region, thus casting light, by implication, on the givers of $500 and up as a group.

The Standard Metropolitan Statistical Area of Cleveland, Ohio, as defined by the Office of Management and Budget, consists of four contiguous counties —Cuyahoga, Geauga, Lake, and Medina—containing a central city of 751,000 people (1970) and a total population of just over 2 million. It has the twelfth largest population among U.S. metropolitan areas.

63 Occupational information for Cleveland area givers was derived initially from several city directories. These were the Cleveland Directory Company's *Cleveland City Directory 1968, Cleveland East Suburban Directory 1968, Cleveland West Suburban Directory 1968,* and directories for earlier years; and R. L. Polk and Company's *Painesville–Mentor City Directory 1971.* Supplementary sources were the *1968 Dun and Bradstreet Million Dollar Directory* (New York: Dun & Bradstreet, Inc., 1967) and *Standard and Poor's Register of Corporations, Directors and Executives, United States and Canada, 1968* (New York: Standard and Poor's Corporation, 1968).

64 Seventy-seven percent of the Cleveland givers were corporate officers and/or directors. Most of them had multiple occupations. Various combinations of attorney, vice-president, president, director, and chairman of the board were common within firms and, in 60 percent of the cases, across firms. Interestingly, a majority of the 178 identified big givers lived in the suburb of Shaker Heights (or, to be more precise, had their "city" residences in the exclusive sections of that beautiful and expensive preserve). Only four had residential addresses in the city of Cleveland. Evidently those who occupy urban offices, control American industry, and contribute big money to the electoral process seldom

need to actually see the real physical and human consequences of the workings of their industrial economy. In their personal lives they can be literally surrounded by beauty and art in an urban landscape that is increasingly ugly and artless.

65 C. Wright Mills, *The Power Elite* (New York: Oxford University Press, 1956), p. 131.

66 *Ibid.,* p. 289.

67 Carol J. Loomis, "A Squeeze on the Directors," *Fortune* (May 15, 1969), 150.

"Top" corporations are those in *Fortune's* directories of the biggest 1,000 industrial corporations and the biggest 50 each of banks, utilities, transportation companies, retailing companies, and insurance companies.

68 *Business Week* (August 22, 1972), 23.

69 G. William Domhoff has shown that there is a national social upper class based on the corporate rich in his two books *Who Rules America?* (Englewood Cliffs, N.J.: Prentice-Hall, 1967) and *The Higher Circles* (New York: Random House, 1970). In the later book, Domhoff used five indicators of the upper class. The use of all five indicators to determine whether a person is in the upper class presupposes exhaustive information about the wealth, schooling, and social affiliations of people and their spouses, siblings, and parents. Despite these difficulties, we were able to use two of the five indicators for Cleveland big givers on our list. These were listings in *The Social Register* for Cleveland and memberships in exclusive clubs (for Cleveland these were correctly identified by Domhoff as the Chagrin Valley Hunt Club and the Union Club). Memberships in clubs were obtained from *The Cleveland Blue Book* (Cleveland, 1970). Even using only two of the five indicators and restricting ourselves to "contributors" themselves (husband-wife combinations and children living at home), 53 percent of the big Cleveland givers were members of the social upper class.

We also employed a purely economic indicator of membership in the corporate rich, counting the names of businessmen who were directors or officers of the biggest 1,000 industrial corporations, the top 50 each of banks, retail companies, utilities, transportation companies, and insurance companies, and a small number of other companies equivalent in size. The source for the lists of corporate rankings was *Fortune,* (May 15, 1969), 166–197, and *Fortune* (June 15, 1970), 120–125. Forty-six percent of the givers were in the corporate lists. The number of contributors in both the social and the corporate lists was 113, or 63 percent of the identified givers. These 113 gave, collectively, 70 percent of all money contributed by the entire group of 178 ($261,000 out of $370,300).

70 Contributions from Cleveland ruling-class members ranged from a dozen at the CFR list's cutoff point of $500, to one at $47,000.

71 The corporate rich are, of course, only part of the business class. The corporate rich, as defined in Chapter Two, are those who own and control the 1,200–1,300 top U.S. corporations and companies, and/or members of the social upper class. The ruling class is relatively small. In the business class as a whole, on the other hand, are millions of people who (subtracting the corporate rich) collectively preside over a minority share of the business system. The vast majority of people in this society are not, of course, in either group. It might be possible, using exhaustive research based on existing lists of givers, to ascertain a dollar size of gift above which most money comes from the corporate rich and below which it does not. To ascertain a dollar size of annual gift at which money coming from the whole business class equals money coming from the rest of the population would probably be much more difficult, since the sought-after point might well occur under the $100 (now, $101) contribution level used in disclosure legislation. Sophisticated survey research might, however, be useful here.

72 Survey Research Center 1968 Election Study.

CHAPTER FOUR

1 G. William Domhoff, *Fat Cats and Democrats* (Englewood Cliffs, N.J.: Prentice-Hall, 1972), p. 28.

NOTES

2   *The New York Times* (October 19, 1972), p. 53.

3   Herbert E. Alexander, *Financing the 1968 Election* (Lexington, Mass.: Heath, 1971), p. 73.

4   *The New York Times* (March 3, 1972), p. 1.

It should be made clear that ITT is bipartisan. The man who became treasurer of the Democratic National Committee after George McGovern's 1972 convention victory, Donald Petrie, was the chairman of an ITT subsidiary and a former partner in the powerful banking and investment house of Lazard Frères and Company, which arranges mergers for ITT and other giant corporations. Even more interestingly, ITT director Felix Royhatn, the principal who had met secretly with Justice Department officials in the negotiations that led to ITT's getting off the antitrust hook, was an early big financial backer of Edmund S. Muskie's campaign for the 1972 nomination; *The New York Times* (March 27, 1972), p. 26. Royhatn was also a Lazard Frères partner.

5   Morton Mintz and Jerry S. Cohen, *America, Inc.* (New York: Dial Press, 1971), pp. 188–189.

6   Walter Pincus, "Silent Spenders in Politics—They Really Give at the Office," *New York* (January 31, 1972), 37–45.

Republic Steel is one of the corporations known to have such an unpublicized contributing program. We did not attempt to uncover the details of the fund, but in our Cleveland study we did come across additional evidence of the political largesse of the corporate team of the Cleveland-headquartered firm. Thirteen officers and directors were on record as having given a total of $46,500 to national political committees (considering only gifts of $500 or more) in 1968. In the Cleveland study Republic was only one of several firms from which several partners, officers or directors, had made big national contributions. The middle-management dunning programs probably shade off at the top of the corporate hierarchy into gifts contributed by several people who happen to share control of the given company.

7   Mintz and Cohen, *op. cit.*, p. 186.

8 *Dollar Politics* (Washington, D.C.: Congressional Quarterly, 1971), pp. 36–38.

9 Dennis M. Callahan, "Partial List of Contributors to U.S. Representative J. William Stanton's 1970 Campaign, Indicating their Association with Certain Banking and Business Interests," unpublished 1972 paper.

10 *The Plain Dealer* (November 2, 1970), p. 11A.

11 *The New York Times* (May 25, 1972), p. 28.

12 See Mintz and Cohen, *op. cit.,* pp. 160–161.

13 In a 1959 survey 70 percent of a sample of top businessmen said their firms urged employees to register and vote. See Dan H. Fenn, "Business and Politics," *Harvard Business Review* (May–June 1959), 8.

14 See James K. Pollock, Jr., *Party Campaign Funds* (New York: Alfred A. Knopf, 1926), p. 65, or Louise Overacker, *Money in Elections* (New York: Macmillan, 1932), p. 181.

15 Overacker, *op. cit.,* p. 141.

16 Louise Overacker, *Presidential Campaign Funds* (Boston: Boston University Press, 1946), p. 16.

17 Domhoff, *op. cit.,* p. 18.

18 *Dollar Politics, op. cit.,* p. 32.

19 The amount of money given by the 15 percent to the Democrats amounted to 10 percent of all money going to national-level politics from the reported givers of $500 and up. Several givers contributed to both parties.

20 Sources for background information on the corporate rich big givers discussed in this and the next chapter are: *Dun and Bradstreet Million Dollar Directory 1971* (New York: Dun and Bradstreet, 1970); *Standard and Poor's Register of Corporations, Directors and Executives, United States and Canada, 1972* (New York: Standard and Poor's Corp., 1972); the U.S. Security and Exchange Commission's *Official Summary of Security Transactions and Holdings,* monthly issues from 1969 through mid-1972; Marianna O. Lewis, ed., *The Foundation Directory, Edition 4,* prepared by the Foundation Center (New York: Columbia University Press, 1971); and the *Fortune* Magazine lists of top corporations (issues of May 15 and June 15, 1972). Supplementary sources are specifically noted.

NOTES

Supplementary sources for David Rockefeller were: *The Rockefeller Empire: Latin America* (Berkeley, Calif.: North American Congress on Latin America, 1969); Alexander, *op. cit.*, p. 291; *The New York Times* (August 20, 1972), p. 41; and "The Battle Over $300-Billion in Bank Trusts," *Business Week* (July 24, 1971), 64–67.

21 G. William Domhoff, *The Higher Circles* (New York: Random House, 1970), pp. 112–136.

22 *The New York Times* (October 28, 1967). Quoted in *The Rockefeller Empire, op. cit.*, p. 18.

23 Alexander estimates total actual Rockefeller family 1968 campaign expenditures to have been $6.5 million. *Op. cit.*, p. 26.

24 Litton Industries proxy statement, December 6, 1969.

25 Alexander, *op. cit.*, p. 331.

26 *The New York Times* (March 14, 1972, p. 1; September 25, 1972, p. 42); Alexander, *op. cit.*, p. 304; and Herbert E. Alexander, *Financing the 1964 Election* (Princeton, N.J.: Citizens' Research Foundation, 1966), p. 128.

27 Alexander, *Financing the 1968 Election,* p. 159.

28 Domhoff, *Fat Cats and Democrats,* p. 49.

29 *Ibid.,* p. 45. Domhoff notes that most members of the key "Jewish" investment houses are Republicans, even if many are also Democrats. Unfortunately the book fails to reveal many of the important corporate and political networks and relationships apparently uncovered, and is generally uninformative on methods used in what must have been an enormous research effort. Domhoff found that in 1968, 43 of the delegates and governors of the prestigious American Jewish Congress gave $162,000 to Democratic committees and $92,000 to Republican committees (excluding gifts to Republican Senator Jacob Javits of New York, which would raise the Republican total). (*Ibid.,* p. 61.) Domhoff's argument is not that most elite Jews give to the Democrats, but that most Democratic big money comes from elite Jews. In our study of big Cleveland givers of 1968, we also found that most Democratic money came from Jewish businessmen.

30 "The $400 Million Election Machine," *Newsweek* (December 13, 1971), 26. See also *The New York Times* (July 3, 1972), p. 18; and Herbert E. Alexander, *Money in Politics* (Washington, D.C.: Public Affairs Press, 1972), p. 115.

31 *The New York Times* (September 25, 1972), p. 42.

32 *The New York Times* (May 17, 1971), p. 1.

33 *The New York Times* (March 27, 1972), p. 1.

34 The Council on Economic Priorities, *Efficiency in Death* (New York: Harper and Row, 1970), pp. 90–91. Chairing City Investing's board was Robert Dowling, one of New York City's chief Democratic fund-raisers, who had personally given more than $100,000 in 1968. Dowling also sat on the United Artists board of Directors. See Domhoff, *Fat Cats and Democrats,* p. 58; and Alexander, *Financing the 1968 Election,* p. 275.

35 Overacker, *Presidential Campaign Funds,* p. 41.

36 John S. Saloma, III, and Frederick H. Sontag, *Parties* (New York: Alfred A. Knopf, 1972), p. 107.

37 Domhoff, *Fat Cats and Democrats,* p. 14.

38 Alexander, *Money in Politics,* pp. 105–106.

CHAPTER FIVE

1 See Alexander Heard, *The Costs of Democracy* (Chapel Hill: University of North Carolina Press, 1960), p. 374.

2 See Louise Overacker, *Money in Elections* (New York: Macmillan, 1932), p. 146.

3 See James K. Pollock, Jr., *Party Campaign Funds* (New York: Alfred A. Knopf, 1926), pp. 84–85.

4 Bureau of the Census, U.S. Department of Commerce, *The Statistical Abstract of the United States* (Washington, D.C.: Government Printing Office, 1971), p. 349.

5 James K. Pollock, Jr., *Money and Politics Abroad* (New York: Alfred A. Knopf, 1932), p. 231.

6 See the analysis of war policy-making by Gabriel Kolko, "Power and Capitalism in Twentieth-Century America," in J. David Colfax and Jack L. Roach, eds.,

Radical Sociology (New York: Basic Books, 1971), especially pp. 226–228.

7   *The New York Times* (January 9, 1972), Sec. IV, p. 9.

8   *The New York Times* (January 7, 1972), p. 14.

9   The Council on Economic Priorities, *Efficiency in Death* (New York: Harper and Row, 1970), pp. 102–104.

10 Herbert E. Alexander, *Financing the 1968 Election* (Lexington, Mass.: Heath, 1971), p. 50. Mott had first spent about $100,000 in a public relations campaign designed to get Rockefeller to run.

11 *The New York Times* (June 24, 1972, p. 40; August 23, 1972, p. 29; and September 25, 1972, p. 42).

12 *The New York Times* (March 8, 1972), pp. 1, 27.

13 George McGovern, "On Taxing and Redistributing Income," *The New York Review of Books* (May 4, 1972), 8.

14 G. William Domhoff, *Fat Cats and Democrats* (Englewood Cliffs, N.J.: Prentice-Hall, 1972), p. 38.

15 *Business Week* (August 5, 1972), 50.

16 *Ibid.*

17 *The New York Times* (June 26, 1972), p. 24.

18 *The New York Times* (June 11, 1972, p. 40; February 29, 1972, p. 22; and April 19, 1972, p. 28).

19 *Fortune* (June 1972), 38.

20 *The New York Times* (July 3, 1972), p. 18.

21 *The New York Times* (August 8, 1972), p. 18.

22 *The New York Times* (August 30, 1972), p. 22. McGovern had sounded the same general theme in an earlier interview with *Business Week* in which he opined that "it's the most serious political crisis in the country— the alienation and disaffection of millions of people who are convinced the government is no longer listening to them . . ."; *Business Week* (May 27, 1972), 69.

23 This conclusion is supported by a survey of voters in the 1972 Democratic primaries in Florida, Pennsylvania, and Wisconsin, conducted by *The New York Times* and Daniel Yankelovich, Inc. See *The New York Times* (April 28, 1972), p. 23.

24 One of several McGovern fund-raising letters received, several times each, by the author in fall 1972. The lists

of names to which these letters were sent were hardly designed to tap the masses. "It doesn't matter whether you can give only $5 or can afford $1,000," one letter reassured the reader. The lists were based on subscription lists for liberal magazines, lists of previous givers, and other such selective sources.

25   *The New York Times* (November 26, 1972), p. 42.

26   An adaptation, for precision's sake, of Domhoff's term "sweet-talking Democrats"; *op. cit.,* p. 176.

27   For the 1968 amount, Alexander, *op. cit.,* p. 194. The actual 1936 amount was $770,000, but we adjusted our comparison for price inflation. Louise Overacker, *Presidential Campaign Funds* (Boston University Press, 1946), p. 50.

28   Harlan Hahn, "Correlates of Public Sentiments About War: Local Referenda on the Vietnam Issue," *The American Political Science Review,* LXIV (December 1970), 1190.

29   See Lewis Chester, Godfrey Hodgson, and Bruce Page, *An American Melodrama* (New York: Viking Press, 1969), pp. 707–710.

30   Quoted in Morton Mintz and Jerry S. Cohen, *America, Inc.* (New York: Dial Press, 1971), p. 158.

31   We calculate that, on the basis of reports filed in conformity with federal law plus other information received by Alexander (*op. cit., passim*), about $35 million came from national-level givers of $500 and over in 1968, excluding secret giving, contributions in kind, and gifts in the under-$500 range.

On the subnational level, unions' inputs of about a tenth of Democratic party receipts for statewide campaigns in Michigan in 1956 and about a quarter of Democratic receipts for analogous races in Wisconsin for 1964 are probably indicative of the order of magnitude of labor's financial importance in the few states where it is a major factor in Democratic party politics. See H. Gaylon Greenhill, *Labor Money in Wisconsin Politics, 1964* (Princeton, N.J.: Citizens' Research Foundation, 1970), pp. 24–25.

32 *The New York Times* (June 6, 1972), p. 1.
33 Grant McConnell, *Private Power and American Democracy* (New York: Alfred A. Knopf, 1967), p. 334.

CHAPTER SIX

1 James Burnham, *The Managerial Revolution* (New York: John Day, 1941), p. 25.
2 Fred R. Harris, "The Frog-Hair Problem," *Harper's Magazine* (May 1972), 15.
3 "Statement of U.S. Senator Fred R. Harris, Consumer Federation, January 27, 1972" (release from the Harris office), p. 1.
4 *Congressional Record* (September 30, 1971), p. S 15446.
5 *Congressional Record* (June 26, 1972), p. S 10152.
6 *Congressional Record* (September 30, 1971), p. S 15442.
7 Fred R. Harris, "The Real Populism Fights Unequal Wealth," *The New York Times* (May 25, 1972), p. 45.
8 Noam Chomsky, *At War with Asia* (New York: Vintage, 1970), p. 38.
9 Herbert E. Alexander, *Financing the 1968 Election* (Lexington, Mass.: Heath, 1971), p. 268.
10 Suzannah Lessard, "The Folding of Fred Harris," *Washington Monthly* (January 1972), 7. See also Harris, "The Frog-Hair Problem," 14.
11 Communication from Fred R. Harris, March 1, 1972.
12 Harris, "The Real Populism Fights Unequal Wealth."
13 Lessard, *op. cit.,* p. 5.
14 See the analysis by Lessard, *op. cit.,* especially p. 13.
15 Frank Parkin, *Class Inequality and Political Order* (New York: Praeger, 1971), p. 81.
16 *Ibid.*
17 See Leon Eisenberg, "The *Human* Nature of Human Nature," *Science* (April 14, 1972), 123–128.
18 Penn Kimball, *Bobby Kennedy and the New Politics* (Englewood Cliffs, N.J.: Prentice-Hall, 1968), pp. 178–179.

CHAPTER SEVEN

1 *Financing a Better Election System* (New York: Committee for Economic Development, 1968), back cover. The statement of objectives appears on the back of all CED policy statements.
2 *Making Congress More Effective* (New York: Committee for Economic Development, 1970), p. 19.
3 *Ibid.,* p. 20.
4 *Electing Congress* (New York: The Twentieth Century Fund, 1970), p. iii.
5 *Voters' Time* (New York: The Twentieth Century Fund, 1969), p. 12.
6 *Ibid.,* p. 15.
7 G. William Domhoff, *Fat Cats and Democrats* (Englewood Cliffs, N.J.: Prentice-Hall, 1972), pp. 168–169.
8 On the role of the NCEC in "getting the ball rolling" on election finance legislation, see Robert L. Peabody *et. al., To Enact a Law* (New York: Praeger, 1972), pp. 36 ff.
9 Subcommittee on Communications, Committee on Commerce, United States Senate, *Federal Election Campaign Act of 1971,* May 25, 1971, pp. 92, 95.
10 *Ibid.,* p. 93.
11 *Ibid.,* p. 199.
12 *Ibid.,* pp. 166–167.
13 *Ibid.,* p. 169.
14 Peabody, *op. cit.,* is a history of this political broadcast legislation.
15 David W. Adamany, *Campaign Finance in America* (North Scituate, Mass.: Duxbury Press, 1972), p. 260.
16 *Financing a Better Election System,* p. 20.
17 *Ibid.,* p. 52.
18 *Electing Congress,* p. 16.
19 *Financing a Better Election System,* pp. 21–25.
20 In addition to the above-cited sources see U.S. President's Commission on Campaign Costs, *Financing Presidential Campaigns* (Washington: U.S. Government Printing Office, 1962), and Association of the Bar of the City of New York, *Congress and the Public Trust* (New York: Atheneum, 1970), pp. 273–286.
21 The reader interested in the history of reform proposals

and legislation is referred to Louise Overacker, *Money in Elections* (New York: Macmillan, 1932), pp. 228–248, and Herbert E. Alexander, *Money in Politics* (Washington, D.C.: Public Affairs Press, 1972), pp. 198–229.

22 James K. Pollock, Jr., *Party Campaign Funds* (New York: Alfred A. Knopf, 1926), p. 232.

23 *Ibid.,* p. 233.

24 See Paul A. Woelfl, "Federal Regulation of Political Activity" (unpublished doctoral dissertation, St. Louis University, 1950), pp. 194, 201.

25 *Dollar Politics* (Washington, D.C.: Congressional Quarterly, 1971), pp. 41–43.

26 *The New York Times,* May 4, 1966, p. 26.

27 Quoted in Marvin E. Gettleman and David Mermelstein, eds., *The Great Society Reader* (New York: Random House, 1967), p. 20.

INDEX

INDEX

INDEX

about the author

David Nichols is a political scientist who studied at Clark University, the University of Chicago, and the Massachusetts Institute of Technology, where he received his Ph.D. Since 1966 he has taught American politics and social theory at the University of Connecticut, the University of Massachusetts, and, most recently, Case Western Reserve University.